CHASING BALANCE

PURSUING THE MYTHICAL ART OF WORK-LIFE BALANCE IN TODAY'S DIGITAL WORLD

Traci Synatschk

Copyright © 2018 by Traci Synatschk

All rights reserved.

This book or any portion thereof may not be reproduced or used in any manner whatsoever without the express written permission of the publisher except for the use of brief quotations in a book review.

Printed in the United States of America

First Printing, 2018

ISBN-13: 978-1986231589

ISBN-10: 1986231585

Visit the author's website at http://www.chasingbalancebook.com to order additional copies.

For Eric, who has always been the calm in my storm.

CHASING BALANCE

Table of Contents

FORWARD — 9

WHERE IT ALL BEGAN... — 13

MINDSET MATTERS — 24

BALANCING TELECOMMUTING AND PARENTING – WHY YOU MUST HAVE A SCHEDULE. — 33

10 THINGS YOU NEED TO KNOW IF YOU'RE CONSIDERING ENTREPRENEURSHIP — 41

TO PLAN OR NOT TO PLAN...IS THAT EVEN A QUESTION? — 50

DOES PRODUCTIVITY EXIST OUTSIDE THE OFFICE ENVIRONMENT? — 55

BATCHING YOUR WORK — 56
BUILDING CONFIDENCE IN YOUR OWN DECISIONS — 57
LEARNING THE DIFFERENCE BETWEEN TIME AND MONEY FOR AN ENTREPRENEUR — 62
DEFINING YOUR PRIORITIES — 64
EMBRACE THE TIME WARP — 67

IS WORKING FROM HOME RIGHT FOR YOU? 74

ARE YOU MADE TO WORK FROM HOME? 74
SELLING WORKING FROM HOME TO THE BOSS 79
POTENTIAL PITFALLS 81

ORGANIZATION IS KEY FOR SUCCESS 84

WHERE WILL YOU WORK? 84
SCHEDULES 87
HOW I BUILD MY SCHEDULE 98
DAILY RITUALS 107
FLEXIBILITY 107

WORKING FROM HOME WITH KIDS 112

IT NEEDS TO BE DONE RIGHT NOW…OR DOES IT? 118
WHAT DOES A TYPICAL DAY LOOK LIKE? 122
SUMMER SCHEDULES 130
VOLUNTEERING…THE THIRD JOB 143

USING TOOLS AND TECH TO FIND YOUR BALANCE 157

FINANCIAL TOOLS 175

THE ART OF BALANCE 207

IS WORK-LIFE BALANCE A MYTH? 207

ABOUT THE AUTHOR 212

Forward

Eleven years ago, I made a bold, scary choice that changed my life. I walked into my boss's office for a review with a churning stomach and a pounding heart. I told him that my husband had received an offer to work in Austin, Texas, and that I wanted to relocate and work from home.

And there was silence, crickets, nothing... If you have ever considered giving up the security of the nine-to-five, you are probably familiar with the gut-churning, stomach-dropping feeling that hit me then. Looking back, it was in that moment that my path as an entrepreneur solidified. I mean no disrespect to the thousands of amazing bosses and companies, including the one I worked for, but there is something so empowering about the ability to make life-altering decisions for yourself without the need for someone else's approval or justification.

But back to the story. A few minutes of uncomfortable silence passed. That horrible, awkward silence where you don't know where to look or what to do. While I was mentally updating my resume, my boss finally broke the silence and told me we could try telecommuting for a short period and see what happens. His response was not enthusiastic. I left his office with the answer I wanted, but it was an empty victory. I did not feel optimistic about his support, even though I strongly believed this was a great move for myself and the company. It was made very clear that this was to be an experiment with no room for me to mess up. I had a bad feeling that I had just slipped down a few rungs on the corporate ladder I had been racing up.

Are you a teen innovator who hopes to never work a day in the corporate world? Or maybe you are a stay-at-home mom looking to get back into the workforce after a long absence. Perhaps, you are a diehard nine-to-fiver who wants a more flexible arrangement. Whatever your motivation might be, telecommuting, either for yourself or someone else, can seem like the perfect answer.

Over the last thirteen years, I have experienced the good, the bad, and the ugly that comes with working from home. This book is a compendium of tips, tricks, strategies, and stories from my journey. I've chronicled over a decade of best practices and productivity hacks that I use to be productive and efficient when working from home! I have juggled corporate work and entrepreneurial pursuits while raising kids and living life, and I understand the desire to find work-life balance and success. I hope my story inspires you to see how productivity strategies and routines can make telecommuting work for you.

Where It All Began...

Working from home can be amazing, and it can also be disastrous! When I first considered working from home, I was about five months pregnant and was starting to struggle with a few pregnancy complications. Around that time, my company was moving offices and we ran into buildout complications that resulted in some tight quarters, and boy do I mean tight! Try fitting an office of 7 employees, cubicles, copy machines, water coolers, desk chairs and filing cabinets into a 10x20 room! I jumped at the chance to work from home! The plan was for this to be a temporary situation until the delayed office construction wrapped up. My advancing pregnancy made it an easy decision to have my office remotely.

Working from home opened a door that would tantalize me for the next few months, as I tried to figure out how to balance motherhood and work. Like many first-time moms to be, I was unexpectedly conflicted. I was torn between loyalty to everything I had worked for in my career and terror at feeling like I would miss out on all motherhood had to offer if I wasn't there for the magical moments featured in every baby-centric TV commercial.

Turns out I wasn't alone. As I visited daycare after daycare looking at childcare options, I crossed paths with other moms and moms-to-be struggling with the same predicament. We all asked the same questions. Do we try to live on one income to avoid childcare costs? Do we work to pay for childcare? So many people, moms, dads, adoptive and foster parents, struggle with this monumental decision when trying to figure out how to balance work and family life.

In many cases, working from home, or telecommuting, begins to look like the perfect answer. I used to joke that working and being a mom was like walking a tightrope. You had buckets on either side full of work and life priorities. Every project at work, every playdate, every doctor's appointment or unexpected work meeting had the potential to unbalance me and tumble me from my precarious perch on the tightrope.

If I didn't keep my buckets balanced, my little world was going to spiral into chaos. As both a natural planner and a soon-to-be mom, that was a scary and stressful thought. It's so hard to find that balance, but the thought is always there, tempting us all.

I wanted to be 100% at everything I was doing. I wanted to be the best mom, a driven employee, a loving wife, an engaged best friend, but it's not possible to be 100% of everything all the time. Something had to give.

I knew that I didn't want to read a piece of paper each day giving me a 10-second report on my child's day. I didn't want to read a memo documenting what he had eaten, or a one liner if I had missed any major milestone like his first word...I wanted to see it all! I wanted to be there for it all. I wanted to tackle parenthood with the same devotion I had applied to my marriage, my job, and my life up to this point.

I also knew that I was good at my job, and I gained a lot of joy and confidence from it. This is the dirty little secret. Some of us like to work. We don't flee the office because we're lazy, unmotivated individuals who plan to camp on the couch in pajamas watching TV all day.

> You might be reading this thinking, hold on, this book's all about parenthood and that doesn't apply to me, but that's only half right. Balancing parenthood and work was my driving force, my why. It was the reason I needed to consider working from home. Your why might be very different, but knowing what drives you and why telecommuting is a potential solution is very important. It will help you keep your focus when the going gets rough...and believe me some days, the going will get rough.

We flee because we're asked for more than anyone can really give these days. Higher prices for homes, groceries, and childcare lead to the need for two-income families. Two-income families lead to the struggle to balance work and home. It's a vicious circle. My husband and I had just bought a house, we had a car payment, and I was just starting to pay off the loans that came with my great college education (sic 'em Bears). On the outside, we were the very typical picture of a young family just starting out. On the surface, everything was great, but when I dug deeper, I realized I was seriously conflicted.

When we're used to being able to create the reality we want, it's difficult to realize that sacrifice is still so much a part of life. If you want to go on a great vacation, you might have to trade the huge house. If you want the fancy big house, you might have to trade being a stay-at-home parent. If you want to be at home and quit your job, you have to be willing to sacrifice some luxuries and live on one income.

Everything is about balance, about trade-offs. The question is, what are you willing to trade?

When I decided to roll the dice and work from home, I was searching for balance. I had this idea that if I could work early and work late, if I could work around the baby's schedule, I wouldn't miss out. But there's a whole other sacrifice that comes with working from home. You sacrifice your 9-to-5. You sacrifice your early mornings, your weekends, and your evenings in some cases. You give up the ability to walk away from an office at the end of the day. So often in the early days, I felt like I was on call around the clock. Much of that was self-inflicted, as I struggled to prove that I was just as available and just as valuable an employee, even while working from home.

That first year or two that I was working from home, I clocked more hours than I ever had, which says a lot since I frequently put in 60 and 70 hours a week in the early days of my career. I felt like I had something to prove, that I had to show that I was just as valuable a team member now that I wasn't in the same building. That need to prove yourself is both a blessing and a curse...watch out for it. I found that I would worry about things that had never bothered me in the office.

My company has instant messaging, which is an amazing tool for telecommuters to stay connected. When I first started working from home, I would panic if my status changed from available to away, even if I was just working with pen and paper. Looking back, my colleagues never felt I was unreachable or out of touch, and never once did someone comment on my instant messaging status. Setting expectations and having open communication with your team is essential to help alleviate stress you may be piling on yourself.

This book is going to talk about routines, organization, structure, and then, ironically, flexibility. Creating balance when working at home takes work and effort. If you go into it without routine, without structure, without organization, you will be overwhelmed. You will always feel compelled to be on the clock because you have something to prove. It becomes so important to incorporate flexibility in your routine when working from home if you hope to find that elusive balance.

The information in this book is intended to help everyone, including entrepreneurs, corporate ladder climbers, direct sales reps, and even college students. When I first started working from home, I was working for a corporate company in a very traditional 9-to-5. After three short years, I made the leap to a full-time telecommuting position in my search for balance. Over the years, I've juggled a thirty-hour corporate work week, my own entrepreneurial business and freelance consulting for startups, in addition to raising three kids.

I attribute a huge amount of my success, and my sanity, to taking action. I am such a believer in making sure you take action that I have launched an entire movement dedicated to it! Find out more on the #EntrepreDOit revolution at www.entrepreDOit.com. Seriously, taking action is EVERYTHING.

One reason we often encounter roadblocks when we try to move forward is a lack of direction on how to get from our WHY to our WHERE. It's really important to make sure that you keep the reasons driving you aligned with your final destination. Make sure that you can get to where you want to be in a week, in a month, in a year and in ten years through the actions you're taking today.

There are so many tips, tricks, and life hacks that can make working from home work. It's not all working in your PJs at noon and fortress of solitude style isolation. Creating a work from home haven is important, and we're going to talk about how to design the lifestyle you've been looking for. I adore working from home and I am a huge advocate for using telecommuting to add hours back into your day. It's a peaceful, productive place for me, and after more than ten years of commuting down the stairs to my office, I'm going to share the systems, schedules and strategies that make it work.

I hope you enjoy this book and are inspired to join the #EntrepreDOit revolution to create the change you've been looking for. I am a real life, tightrope walking, entrepreneurial mom, who is still balancing that 30-hour corporate work-week, juggling my entrepreneurial endeavors (www.MentoringU.org and www.EntrepreDOit.com), and in the weeds with mom life. I practice what I preach in this book, and I am looking forward to sharing what I have learned over the last decade and a half with you.

Mindset Matters

What is mindset? Your mindset is the collection of ideas, assumptions, strategies, and methods that drive the choices you make. Whenever you make a choice, your underlying assumptions influence what choice you make, how you react and how comfortable you are with the outcome.

If your mindset is negative and expecting failure, that is likely to influence your outcome. The systems that I use help me with everything, from developing a routine that doesn't tax my sanity, to working with a baby at home while maintaining my corporate work responsibilities, to making sure that I don't work at all hours, and ensuring that there is time for all my priorities - professional, personal and health. That's a hefty load for a little list! Grab your free sample copy of my priority planner by visiting http://www.chasingbalancebook.com/bonus.

Why Mindset Matters

We hear a lot about mindset these days. In writing this book, I spent some time pondering why it pops up more and more in conversation, on social media and in coaching. I've come to the conclusion that in days gone past, we had a more graceful existence. We cooked, we sewed, we built...we created. Over time, we have industrialized so many parts of our society, created a profit-driven workaholic culture and idealized financial success. Along the way, we seem to have lost the element of creation that used to be a part of daily life.

These days, we flock to Pinterest, ohh and ahh over what crafty mums have done and decide what projects to DIY over the weekend. We've turned creating, building, and entertaining into an artistic hobby. It's no longer the norm for an elegant dinner party with dressed up guests to be a regular part of our lifestyle. We don't seem to slow down long enough. Perhaps, I am alone, but the grace we've lost along the way nags at me.

We have seen small businesses on the rise and Entrepreneurship seems to be the topic on the tip of everyone's tongue lately. I think this is a natural result of our need to create. We build businesses the way we use to build dog houses as children - a weekend idea that morphs into a project, and before Monday rolls around, we have a name, a URL and a website. We have a driving need to say I DID THIS. I created something, I've left my mark and have something to show for it.

Entrepreneurship fills a void we have not consciously known was missing. We pursue that which we need and didn't even recognize was missing. For myself, and perhaps you, being an entrepreneur allows us to merge what we are good at and what we want to accomplish in a way that the traditional 9-5 cannot. I love Entrepreneurship and the opportunities it presents. I love the satisfaction of building something...creating a website, a dining room table (see the sidebar for my latest hands on project) or a truly exceptional meal.

We move at such a hectic pace these days, shuffling from school drop-offs to work, to after-school extracurriculars to the dinner rush, before we finally collapse at the end of the night and allow Netflix and wine to erase the stress of the day. Life is hard, balance is hard, parenthood is hard and taking time to slow down and immerse ourselves in something new is difficult. However, *Hard Work* is not something to shy away from. We need to lean in and embrace what challenges us, what stretches our comfort zone and, in the end, what fulfills us.

Successfully seeing an idea through to fruition builds confidence. How often have you wanted to try something and held back because you didn't know if it would work, if it would come out just right. If you have ever held off on starting something because of the fear of failure, your mindset was affecting your outcome.

Sometimes taking action leads to failure and sometimes it leads to greatness, but consistently taking action is the only way to build your confidence and begin to change your mindset. If you try something once and fail, that doesn't mean you should stop, it means you should try it another way. Over time, pushing yourself to take action on your ideas, your dreams, your priorities, will lead to a more positive mindset that will support your efforts and begin to influence the success you have!

> *Questions to ask yourself:*
> - *Are you ready to be your own boss?*
> - *Are you looking for a way to balance work and kids?*
> - *Do you have a passion for what you do?*
> - *Do you have good organizational skills?*
> - *Are you able to prioritize?*
> - *Are you ready to invest in yourself to make your dreams happen?*
>
> *Entrepreneurship - it's the dream for more and more people these days. We live in a world that continues to devalue the personal approach to business. It's all about the sale, the profits, with little regard to loyalty, and longevity.*

It's a weird system we've created, where we look at college and a good job as proof of a successful life and promising future. We have a slew of schools where we guarantee application to and acceptance at a 4-year college. My children attend a charter school where they proclaim a 100% acceptance to college rate and they use this as one of their strongest selling points.

This is the path we set our children upon…but how many of us reading this book are paying off school debt while struggling to start, launch and grow a business?

I know I am.

I received an amazing education and it definitely shaped who I am today. But looking back, I wish I had seen the fork in the road, the place where I could have detoured from the societal norm and pursued an idea, a dream. I'm not knocking college by any means, but my mindset at the time was that there was a very specific road to success. The formula was simple…graduate from high school, go to a great college, get a good job. Turns out, that isn't the only way.

> *I use an action-oriented planner built to guide me through 90-day segments where I think through my goals, my priorities and my path.*
>
> *You can grab a free download of the priority planner at <http://www.chasingbalancebook.com/bonus>.*
>
> *Use the planner to help identify what your priorities are and what actions you need to take to support and sustain them.*
>
> *Annual big picture planning can be very useful in figuring out what you want to accomplish and work toward. Breaking your big picture plan into 90-day segments so you can identify actionable goals is essential to creating accountability and staying on track. Taking those goals and tracking your progress on monthly and weekly increments helps you build success.*

Many Entrepreneurs don't find the confidence or determination to strike out on their own until a tipping point occurs and their mindset changes. For some, it's starting a family and re-prioritizing where they see their future. For others, it's the moment they realize that the path they are pursuing doesn't bring them the joy they are looking for. For many, there is a desire to create something, build something. That desire often drives us to create a side hustle, or turn a passion into a profitable business enterprise. In some cases, it comes as necessity with job loss or an intolerable work situation. Whatever the tipping point is for you, make sure you spend some time thinking about what is driving you and where you want this road to take you. Develop a mindset that focuses on a positive outcome and reinforce it with actions you can take to see it through.

Balancing Telecommuting and Parenting – Why you must have a schedule.

> *Did you know that U.S. workers actually spend more time commuting to work than vacationing each year? How depressing is that?*
>
> *If I still lived in Dallas and commuted just 25 miles round trip into the office, Commuter Challenge estimates that my commuting costs me $3821.04 per year. I could do a lot of things with $3800 dollars! Makes me glad I work from home, have my kids at a school right down the street and only need to fill my minivan up once every three weeks or so.*
>
> *When you are determining if telecommuting is a good fit for you, don't forget to analyze the monetary savings it can bring you.*

We all have routines. Some of us get up in the morning and head off to work out before the sun is up. Some of us don't feel like the day has started until that first cup of coffee is in hand. One pillar of my success is creating structure and routine that ensures I have my bases covered when it comes to work and home life. When trying to balance competing priorities, it becomes so important to make sure that I'm not adding any additional stress to my workload that could be avoided with some simple attention to detail.

Having an overactive toddler, two school-aged kids, and a husband who travels makes me one grateful momma that I work from home. Yes, it's a challenge, and I hear time and time again that I couldn't do that, I would be too distracted. Well, not to revert back to mimic my toddler, but "can't never could." It takes effort, but so does leaving the office group chit-chatting around the copy machine to go meet a deadline in an office. As a very social person, I actually get more done at home without the social distractions of visiting with peers.

I have also, over my last 2 pregnancies, had multiple opportunities to be grateful that I could clock my hours in a flexible fashion. In some days during my pregnancy, a nap was essential to making it through the day. And on other days, I was too sick to work first thing in the morning. Working from home allowed me to work when I was best able to and not be held to a 9-5 mentality when the quality of my work wouldn't have been nearly as good.

When you first start working from home, you might find it tough to establish a workable routine. It might be hard to differentiate work time from home time and work to-do lists from personal to-do lists on days when you feel like you never want to leave the house. The exercise below will help you come up with a workable routine that can help you get started.

Building Your Routine

Grab a sheet of paper, or head over to http://www.chasingbalancebook.com/bonus to grab your daily routine planner worksheet. Work your way through the following steps to get started building a great routine to support you.

1. Make a list of things you do when you are at home and not working. Do you do the dishes, sweep the floors, work out, start a load of laundry? What do you do to start your day?

2. Make a similar list of things you do when you are working. When you get to the office, do you grab a cup of coffee, tidy your desk, check your email?

3. Make a list of anything that distracts you from doing work. For instance, I can't work in a messy space. If my

desk is cluttered, I have to clean it before I can concentrate.
4. What hours do you plan to work?
5. When do you plan to work out?
6. Are there any blocks of time that you plan to be offline/unavailable regularly?
7. Take a fresh sheet of paper, or use page 2 of your bonus download and start aligning your work and home schedules. An example of mine is below. You'll see that it's a blend of work and life activities, so I have dedicated windows of each blended together.

> *An Inside Look at My Schedule*
> *5:00am - Wake up & Work out on walking desk while checking email*
> *6:00am - Review today's top 3 list, check today's schedule and note any high-priority meetings/calls*
> *6:30am - Shower and tidy bathroom/master bedroom*
> *7:00am - Wake everyone up, coffee, breakfast, kitchen cleanup*
> *7:45am - School drop-off*
> *8:15am - 2nd cup of coffee, re-check emails, start on top 3 list*
> *9:00-2:00 - Flexible schedule. Priority on work, specifically top 3 list, meetings and calls*
> *2:00 - Shutdown work for the day, review tomorrow's schedule, make top 3 list, House tidy, dinner prep*
> *3:00 - School pickup*
> *4:00 - Homework, play with the kids*
> *5:00 - Make Dinner*
> *6:00 - Dinner - Family Style*
> *7:00 - House Tidy, Baths, Stories, Bedtime Routines*
> *8:00 - Kids in bed, R&R*

Once you have created a potential schedule, try it out. It will take a few days to work out the kinks, but eventually the schedule should match your natural routines enough that it's a good guide but not something you have to continually refer to. As you get more embedded in your schedule, you might find other things you need to add. If you find yourself jumping right into work and not leaving your chair until lunch, make sure you build breaks and meals into your routine.

I'm a big advocate of incorporating fitness and health into your routine because it is way too easy when you work from home to become more sedentary than usual. Personally, I'm a big fan of the Pomodoro Technique, where you work for focused periods and then take a break before beginning another focused session. Using the Pomodoro technique ensures that I take a break every half hour or so. I use this to clear my head, move around and drink some water. Days when I skip this strategy I find myself feeling stiff, tired and hungry when I finally remember to stand up and move around.

Balancing home life and telecommuting poses challenges, but some upfront planning and a schedule you can stick with can go a long way to making the situation work for you.

10 Things You Need to Know if You're Considering Entrepreneurship

If you find yourself pondering Entrepreneurship, for personal, financial or any other reason, there are a few things you should know.

ONE - It's not easy, but it is worth it. Never be afraid of hard work. Something that seemed so natural a few generations ago, revered and considered a key part of a good work ethic has become a challenge to circumvent. We hear things like "Work Smart, Not Hard" and rather than being a force for efficiency, it becomes a mantra for those trying to find the easiest way to get a job done. I am not opposed to that, but there are many times when hard work is the shortest route to achieve your goal. Spending 45 minutes searching google for an example of the best way to write an email (we've all done it) might have been spent buckling down and just writing that email.

TWO - You can do it all, but you shouldn't. I am a Do It Yourself (DIY) gal at heart. I have taught myself Photoshop, illustrator, and countless other pieces of software so I could save the money and create what my business needs. In the beginning, when I had more time than money, this was usually a decent strategy. But looking back, I wonder how much faster my business would have grown if I had been marketing instead of designing logos, business cards and websites. I could find and work with great people for affordable prices (Fiverr, anyone?). But back then, and still today, I am the best at marketing my business and securing my future success.

One thing many startup entrepreneurs overlook is the value of outsourcing from the very beginning.

THREE - Time spent planning is an investment. Mind Mapping, business planning, goal setting; these are all planning tools that often get brushed aside during the startup phase. They are seen as something we will get to one day, **but** that day rarely comes. These tools can be essential to identifying your ideas, narrowing your niche and creating strategies for success. Don't shortchange yourself by skipping over them.

FOUR - Big or small, you need a business plan, or better yet, a Business Roadmap. Business plans don't have to be 100 pages with charts, graphs and endless financial worksheets. Business planning, or Roadmapping, is an exercise where you put pen to paper and make sure your idea has merit. Developing a solid business plan can serve as your validation of your ideas and can create a roadmap for your business for years to come. Check out the book's online resources section for a free business roadmap template and guide (http://www.chasingbalancebook.com/bonus).

FIVE - Surround yourself with positive supporters, but listen objectively to the naysayer. We have all been there. You have an idea that has you dancing around, talking excitedly to anyone who will listen, and ready to take on the world...and then you talk to a Debby Downer who rains on your startup parade and immediately has you doubting your future as an entrepreneur. When you are launching a business, one of the best moves you can make is to find a group of like-minded individuals who can support you on your journey. They will help keep your motivation up, help you work through any issues and be a sounding board for future ideas. They will be your safe harbor when it feels like success is so very far away. Find refuge from your doubts with them, let their enthusiasm feed yours and keep you motivated, but occasionally invite in constructive criticism. Don't be afraid of the naysayer...just don't let them derail you! Understand that the very best idea still won't be successful unless there is a market for it.

SIX - Develop an inspiration board and at least 3 affirmations. When the going gets tough, the entrepreneur needs to remember why they got started. What was their driving factor, their tipping point moment, their WHY. Create a visual that can be printed, framed, laminated, or tattooed on your arm. Just kidding about the tattoo, unless that's your jam, but the rest is solid advice! Keep it handy and look at it each day. Find at least 3 affirmations that help create positive connotations with your goals. Say them to yourself, shout them out loud, write them down, or whisper them in the shower...just be mindful and intentional, reminding yourself each day why you are on this path.

SEVEN - Start with the end in mind. Create your systems and stick with them from day one. Review your numbers on Friday, write blog posts on Monday, review social media needs monthly... whatever you determine to be ongoing, regular business needs, carve out time and make them a priority. Think about what your business will look like when you are established and successful, and work backwards to create the organization to support that dream. Use tools like Trello, Asana, and Google Calendar to set up processes and keep you on track. Try out the Productive Entrepreneur Trello Board to get started! (http://www.chasingbalancebook.com/bonus).

EIGHT - Build a business that works for YOU! Building a business, your business... it takes time, effort, late nights, early mornings and more sacrifices than you can imagine. Make sure that you are looking at the business you are creating from every angle. Is this a business you will still be happy running 10 years from now? When you are successful and have achieved your goals, what does that look like and how does the life you want to be living fit in? Don't build a business that needs you in the office 40 hours a week if you don't want to be in the office for 40 hours per week.

NINE - Numbers don't lie. Make it an essential part of your week to review the numbers. Good, bad or ugly, numbers don't lie.

Know if your business is on track, behind or exceeding expectations. Knowledge is essential to success, and knowing how your business is performing is vital to becoming and staying successful. If you're not great at budgeting and tracking finances, use a program or system that does it for you, like quickbooks or waveapps. (http://www.chasingbalancebook.com/bonus).

TEN - See failure as part of the path to success. Few people succeed the first time at building a business. For most, success is a winding road. Try to enjoy the journey, and always view failure as a setback or learning experience. Failure is only a roadblock if you don't detour and find a new way, a new path to achieve your objective. Never stop trying. When I left for college, I was going to be a doctor. By my sophomore year, I was going to be a writer (kind of funny as I write this book!). The next time I was home for vacation and was asked, I admitted that I didn't know. I was exploring my options. The more we learn and explore an idea, the more we refine our interests and find what truly inspires and excites us. Entrepreneurship is a very similar journey, in that for many of us our ideas get refined, our businesses change. It's a living growing entity that sometimes feels like it has a life of its own. Don't be afraid of change!

TO PLAN OR NOT TO PLAN...IS THAT EVEN A QUESTION?

I'm often asked what my secret is, when do I sleep, and how do I get so much done.

Let me preface this by saying that there is no mystery magic secret, just like there is no magic pill for weight loss. Being an action-oriented entrepreneur is the result of planning. There were many long, long, long days. I'm not normally given to pity parties, fits of depression or mindless rants, but some days can bring out the whiny toddler in the best of us. I remember one period early in my working-from-home journey when there were brush fires all around Austin. I had an over-anxious kindergartener, a tyrant toddler determined to overthrow the leadership in our house, and a husband dealing with food poisoning. It was an interesting few days to say the least.

The reality is, this is real life. There is always a sick kid, a crazy work day, and a thousand tasks to get done.

What did I do?

I made time to have some wonderful adult conversations (crazy how 5 minutes conversing with an adult about something non-child related can make me remember that I'm smarter than I feel when buried in a rough patch), had tiramisu ice cream (way to go Blue Bell!) and I hid in a closet to find time to plan and prepare for the upcoming week. I'm a planner by nature, so unplanned, chaotic, willy-nilly reactionary weeks drive me crazy.

To me, the absolute key to successfully working from home and raising kids is planning and organization. Now I know that sounds like a no-brainer, but think about how many times you get up, walk into the office, turn on the computer and respond to whatever email sounds the most urgent. Five hours later, the to-do list you made three days ago still hasn't been touched.

We're a reactionary society, and it's a pitfall that those working from home especially have to be careful to avoid.

When I first started working from home, I was worried that my boss was going to sit in front of his computer around the clock waiting on my IM status to go to "away" and then message me something to try and see if I was really working. Ten years later, and I still feel the need to prove myself worthy of working from home. I used to send emails first thing in the morning so people would know I was on the clock, and I would rarely take a real lunch break. But the funny thing is, for my company at least, results matter far more than the exact minutes I'm in front of the computer.

I've gotten creative with my time as my kids came along. I still work a full day, but it's rarely from 8 a.m. to 5 p.m. That is the real beauty of working from home.

I often work from 5 a.m. to 7 a.m. in a quiet house, knocking out any tasks that I need peace and quiet to think through. Then I take a break, have breakfast with my kids, load them up and take the older two to school.

On the way back, I make work calls or just catch up on my podcasts, my guilty pleasure! I'm usually back in the office between 8:15 and 9:00 and can spend an hour catching up on email and updating my to-do list.

When my youngest goes down for a nap, I'm back to phone calls and any other activities that need a quiet house. I take a quick lunch, and then power through the afternoon until 3 or 4 when I head to the carpool lane to pick my kids from school. I rarely have anything major left to finish at that point, but if I do, I usually do it after 8pm when the kids are in bed.

It can make for a long day, but when the house is quiet, when I have that great cup of coffee and can actually catch my breath and have some perspective, I realize that in a society where two incomes are usually needed, this is a great solution. I have my cake and am eating it too (maybe on the run, but still...).

When I get asked how to balance it all and if it's really possible to work at home with kids, I just smile and say Yes! If you're willing to plan, organize and make specific items a priority, it's absolutely possible and 100% worth it.

Build your own Priority list and Download your Daily Planner template in the book bonuses section at http://www.chasingbalancebook.com/bonus

Does Productivity Exist Outside the Office Environment?

There really is nothing like the flexibility of working from home to increase your productivity. When you really need to get something accomplished, think about what you do. You close your doors, put up a 'Do Not Disturb' sign, and you shut everything else out. When you have a deadline or a priority task, you focus on it so that you can get things done.

We create that environment, establishing solitude that allows us to focus and to increase our productivity. We see this in our offices when doors are closed, we see it on IM or phones when statuses are set to Do Not Disturb. What many don't realize is how much easier this can be when you're working from home... as long as you are specific in your intention.

If you want to leave the office to work from home, regardless of whether it's an occasional day at home, or you are setting up a permanent home office, make sure your productivity doesn't take a hit. Get in the right frame of mind for working from home with some solid productivity hacks.

Batching Your Work

One strategy many productivity experts recommend is identifying key blocks of time to get specific tasks done. One highly recommended strategy is blocking off specific times to tackle email. Most experts recommend only checking email two or three times a day, while most people admit to always having email open. How often are you in the middle of a task and see an email notification? Do you ignore it and keep focused or do you hop over to your email, check the message and end up on a different task as you work to answer the newest issue?

When I was working in the office in the early days of my corporate life, I was working sixty or seventy hours a week. I would get into the office around six-thirty or seven o'clock in the morning. I was leaving the office around five or six o'clock in the evening, and always still felt like I had work to do. I attributed that workaholic state to paying my dues and chalked it up to being in the early days of my career. Later, I realized that a lot of my time each day was spent rationalizing the decisions I was making and the work that I was doing.

Building Confidence in Your Own Decisions

We often talk about collaborative environments, and these can be incredibly beneficial, but sometimes we spend so much time bouncing ideas off of other people that our productivity can suffer. Again, that is not to say that collaborative environments for work don't have a purpose and can't be phenomenally useful, but they can also have these pitfalls where we feel like everything we do needs a second set of eyes, resulting eventually in too many cooks in the kitchen. Over time, I feel like this erodes an employee's ability to work autonomously and begins to truly cause a lack of action.

Entrepreneurs, solopreneurs, and freelancers can experience the opposite effect, where they are so used to being a one-man show that any feedback on their ideas can feel like a personal attack. Mastermind groups, Facebook groups and in-person networking groups are a great middle ground. You can have dedicated time to interact with others and gain valuable feedback and knowledge without relying on others to make a decision.

When I began working from home, I started to recognize when and where I actually needed collaboration. It was only on the really important things, and usually only on the big projects that were still in the design phase. Once I was ready to actually put the idea in motion, I had already worked through the advice I had solicited and moved into action mode, ready to get the project done. In many ways, it was easier to wrap projects up quickly since I didn't have that person in the next cube or office tempting me to put my productivity on hold while I got their opinion on something I was already happy with.

I began to rely more on myself, focusing on my thoughts, my ideas and my opinions. That really resulted in an amazing transition in my career and my confidence. Sometimes we forget that we take on a role, or start a business, or pursue an idea because we're good at something. In a digital world, full of constant feedback (both welcome and unwelcome), it can be hard to make a decision completely on your own merit and have confidence in it.

When I began working from home full-time, it very quickly became apparent what I was good at on my own, and what I really needed a team for. Once I realized how things were shaping up, I could make better use of my time by holding meetings with more structure and goals instead of open-ended brainstorming sessions. I accomplished more, and in the end, I was producing more quality work.

I was feeling happier, calmer and more confident in my work from home role, and not too surprisingly, both my attitude and my accomplishments also caught my boss's attention.

Confidence is such a fickle friend. When you are confident in your ideas and speech, you are much more likely to speak with authority and be taken seriously. As my confidence grew, I began to really specialize in specific areas to support my team that made the most of my talents and skills. This didn't happen overnight, but it was a major turning point once I realized that I didn't want to spend time doing work I wasn't suited for. Honestly, I'm not sure if I would have had the confidence to speak up and voice my thoughts on how my time was being utilized if I hadn't transitioned to working from home and seen the difference in my happiness and stress level when I was working on things that I am good at.

If you are in a similar situation, I encourage you to think about what you are good at, what you love to do and how that skill and passion can be used in your profession. If we are doing something that's not in our zone of genius, something that you can do, but is not your best work, then so much of your actual potential for earnings and accomplishments is being missed.

Learning the Difference between Time and Money for an Entrepreneur

Another way to look at that as an entrepreneur is looking at where you spend your time versus money. Just because you can do something doesn't mean you should. Even if you're good at a task, say creating Facebook Ads, it doesn't mean it's the best use of your time. One of the most important and vital lessons that entrepreneurs have to learn is that you are paying regardless of whether you are spending your time or your money. When you are juggling home life, business, and other competing priorities, it's important to evaluate how you are spending you time. When you have to do any task, you need to ask yourself, would somebody else do it better and faster than you? And if so, what would it cost? Then think about what your time is worth...literally put a dollar amount to it and decide if you should pay in time or money.

Let's stick with our Facebook Ads example. Let's say you need to google how to build a Facebook Ad (whether you are new or experienced at this, the rules and best practices change frequently), create the graphics and copy, figure out Facebook Ad Manager, research and determine how to create and narrow a custom audience, determine the best ad time frame and spend, load the copy and graphics you created and submit the ad. How long would that take you if you were completely focused, didn't get distracted and worked straight through? Maybe 2 hours, 4 hours, or even 1 day? What is one day of your time worth? What else could you do with that day? Could you make phone calls and generate leads? Could you network and make a sale?

There is no 100% correct answer to this question. It's going to depend on your goals, your finances, and your needs. For most businesses, there's a cycle that occurs, where in the beginning you have less money and more time and going the DIY route is the best use of your resources. However, as your business grows, be on the watch for the time when you have both time and money. This is when you need to consider outsourcing or staffing up and need to be wary of micro-managing every detail. In most cases, you sell your business or product better than anyone else and your time should be spent making the sale instead of building the resources that support the sale.

Defining Your Priorities

The crux of the matter is that we have to identify our priorities and use those to ensure we are being productive. As an Entrepreneur, you are the boss and need to have an eye on the big picture. Whether you are managing a team as you grow your business, or you are just working on making the most of you own time, it's essential to know what you are best at, what you are worst at, and what makes a financial difference in your business.

In my business, MentoringU, I often start out client conversations with a discussion on what you are good at, what you aren't good at, and what you specifically do to make money. The idea is to make sure we are not only focusing on what you're good at, but what makes money. If you are great at networking, but all your sales come from holding webinars, then prioritizing networking isn't the best choice.

It became apparent very quickly that I was great at logistics. I was great at pulling together projects and identifying timelines and tasks, then breaking them down and making them run like clockwork. What I wasn't great at was developing the flow charts and visuals that helped demonstrate what was broken down and needed to be fixed. I would get hung up on color schemes and graphic alignment. I would spend a long time creating the visual as I did at solving the issue. As I began to look at prioritizing my time, it was abundantly clear that I needed to hand that portion of the task off to someone who excelled at it, even though that meant building in time to explain what I needed to someone else. In the end, involving another person made me more productive and profitable, even with the additional costs. The time I could now spend doing what I did well that made money outweighed the additional costs and allowed me to level up my entrepreneur game.

Embrace the Time Warp

I also found that the work that used to take me eight or nine hours a day was getting done in five. At first, this was weird and a little disconcerting. Until you are working from home and have built out your daily productivity rituals and routines, it is hard to realize how much time is spent in unproductive work efforts at the office, or at least it was for me!

We've all heard about 'water cooler chats' and breakroom distractions. When I worked in the office, it was a small office, and hanging out by the water cooler/breakroom didn't happen quite so much as wanting feedback on an idea. So you popped by someone's office and ended up there for two hours re-doing the work you just completed to include new ideas that you and the officemate came up with together. I always considered myself a productive team member, but never realized how much my reliance on team feedback was affecting how much I could get done.

When I was pregnant with my first baby, and home on modified bedrest, it hit me (and haunted me later) how much time I would have for personal priorities and family life if I took back all those moments I spent in unproductive pursuits throughout the day. All the time spent in meetings that don't lead anywhere, the time spent re-doing tasks because an idea or a need wasn't communicated well, and even the time spent fighting the massive printer I nicknamed sloth at our office...all that wasted time became an issue when I had new priorities to balance. When I went from career girl working my way up the ladder to excited future mom determined not to miss out, everything changed.

When people say everything changed, what they really mean is that their priorities changed. Something rocked the boat and now it's time to reassess what matters and how it's all going to work together. When I looked at my work and personal life as a whole, I knew I didn't want to spend two hours in the car commuting every day, see my traveling husband each weekend, and try to work motherhood in. I wanted to shake things up and let them resettle in a more balanced way. For me, that path started with working from home so I could be more productive on my work tasks and have more of myself for family.

According to companies hiring remote workers, there are certain skills they look for when hiring remote workers. The good news is that people may already have some of these skills, and the others are fairly easy to learn.

Sidebar: Welchs Survey

According to <u>Working Mother</u>, <u>Welch's Grape Fruit Juice</u> commissioned a study of 2,000 women and found that the average mom spent 98 hours (98!) each week working at the office and taking care of things at home. According to the results, the average mom's day starts at 6:23 a.m. and ends at 8:31 p.m. — that's a total of about 14 hours! The average mom only gets one hour and seven minutes of free time every day. On top of a non-stop routine is the ever-present pressure to feed and fuel the whole family – nearly three quarters of moms (72 percent) feel getting their family to eat healthy snacks and meals is a real struggle.

The reasons behind that struggle? Family members being picky eaters and struggling to find something the whole family enjoys were cited as leading causes of difficulty when it comes to feeding the whole family. On top of that is the pressure to keep things healthy – and eight in ten moms (83 percent) feel pressure to include fruit and vegetables in their family's diet.

The same can be said for drinks, with nearly two thirds (64 percent) of moms struggling to find beverages for the family that they are confident are nutritious and healthy.

Aside from your ability to do the actual job, employers want applicants for their remote jobs to demonstrate these skills:

- *Digital communication skills: verbal and written*
- *Time management, task management, the ability to self-focus*
- *Proactive communication: being comfortable speaking up and asking questions*
- *Comfort with technology and troubleshooting basic technical issues*
- *[Growth mindset](): embracing change and learning*
- *Familiarity with remote communication tools like IM, video conferencing, file sharing, and virtual office environments*

Finding balance is about knowing your priorities and realizing that each day you need to make time for what's important. On some days, all I need to do is work, and on other days, it's a blend of work and family priorities. When you identify your key priorities, and by key, I mean a short list that can actually be tackled, you can focus on the important, must-get-done stuff first.

I joke that balance is a mythical art, a bit of behind the curtain hocus-pocus and sleight of hand. Sometimes it feels like that because of all the life hacks and technology that I use to support my system. However, when you look at studies that show that most working women say that they only get 1 hour and seven minutes on average of time to themselves every day, the minutes begin to add up. I found that when I was really focused, I was accomplishing everything I had done before with less stress, in less time, and that was the holy grail to me. At the end of the day, that's what I was looking for... just a little balance in my life. I wasn't trying to walk away from my career, I wasn't trying to slack off on my contributions at work, or to our financial budget at home; I was just looking for a way to take my life back. A way to have the time that I was spending sitting in traffic day in and day out, and use it in a way that mattered more to me. Working from home really made that happen, especially when my productivity shot up and the time I was spending on work ramped down.

Is Working from Home Right For You?

If you are thinking about pitching your boss on the benefits of your working from home, make sure that it aligns with your priorities for work and life. When you are framing the discussion with your employer, or if you're an entrepreneur and you are just looking to start a business and you want to establish some productive best practices for working from home, take a minute to think about whether your strengths and weaknesses are going to be of help or a hindrance at home.

Are You Made to Work from Home?

I'm a firm believer that anyone can learn productivity, but certain personality traits will make working from home easier.

Self-motivation is key. If you're the type of person who can think about a task, make a list of what needs to be done to accomplish that task, set aside the time to work on it, and follow through to your end result, you're self-motivated. Self-motivation is critical when working from home because whether you're the boss, or whether you have a boss, they need to know that the job is going to get done. This is especially important if you're an entrepreneur because, often, entrepreneurs don't have anyone there to motivate them.

No one is going to force them to tackle the parts of their work that they don't want to do. Maybe as an entrepreneur you love social media and are more than happy to spend hours each day developing social media graphics and posting on various social media sites. It's all marketing, right? But you hate dealing with money and clients and so you wait to invoice your clients for work that you've done. Do you see how that could be financially detrimental to your business all because you didn't prioritize and you weren't self-motivated to do task that needed to get done. Doing our favorite tasks can be easy and often isn't the issue.

Communication skills are also essential. Being able to communicate via phone, email, instant message, or even smoke signals is also an essential skill. When you're working from home, so much of the trust and confidence that are needed for a team comes with the knowledge that you're working on the right activities, that you and your team are on the same page, and moving toward the same goal. That knowledge is built through communication. If you are not communicating with your team and letting them know what you're working on, status updates on your projects, even issues you encounter, then it's very hard to move projects forward with a remote worker. If you're an entrepreneur, communication is still essential. You control your financial success, your marketing success, everything...it's all on you. If you are not communicating with clients clearly, you might suffer financially.

Initiative is another trait that those who excel at working from home are often gifted with. Think about what happens when you encounter an issue. Do you let it stop you until you can reach out to a boss or a co-worker for assistance? Do you turn to research and check Google or online resources? Are you good at coming up with ideas on how to solve the problem on your own? Some problems need expert advice or the voice of experience, but many just need a quick Google search. Remote workers with initiative are often seen as self-motivated problem solvers because they handle problems on their own unless they need to be escalated.

Finally, confidence is a trait that will serve you well working from home. As we talked about earlier, confident people are more likely to voice their ideas, are more likely to be listened to, and are more likely to be seen as a vital part of the team. I found that my confidence grew as I began working from home because I explored more of my own thoughts instead of constantly soliciting other people's input into concepts that I was developing.

As an entrepreneur, always remember that your confidence inspires confidence. If you don't present yourself and your product or your work with confidence, it's very difficult for consumers to think you're going to be able to solve their problems.

Selling Working from Home To the Boss

Once you decide that working from home is the right fit for you, it's time to think about how to make the transition happen. If you currently work in a traditional office, an employer is going to be interested in your productivity and whether it's going to go up or down. They're going to be interested in your financial cost. Is working from home going to cost them more or less than if you were working in the office? They're going to be interested in how you are going to stay on top of meeting with the team so that teamwork and collaboration doesn't suffer. Believe me when I tell you that there are so many tools to make that easy. I might just be the queen of techie tools in the land of new-age tech! Crown me now.

For a full list of my favorite tech to support working at home, be sure to check out www.chasingbalancebook.com/bonus.

There are several resources mentioned in the bonus section, but here I'll cover a few of my favorites. It's an online video conferencing that allows a gallery view so you can see everybody's video all at the same time, a whiteboard and screen sharing, and use it free for team meetings up to forty minutes. It's a great way to be able to very quickly do brainstorming, team collaboration or even troubleshooting to work out the kinks in a project for any team. If you do corporate work and have company solutions, those often work too, but realize that there is free or affordable tech for everyone, so staying in touch with a team is not an impediment to any situation.

You can still have a little bit of that water cooler chat time and team building camaraderie and really make sure that you don't feel isolated from the team. There is a plethora of tools that support team communication, project management, and productivity that you can use, many of which are absolutely free. I am a vocal advocate of leveraging tech to support your success. The end goal is always for work-life balance through better productivity. So keep in mind that if you are planting the seed or having an open conversation with yourself or an employer, the strongest selling points for working from home can be the cost savings and that you have skill sets that make you ideally suited for working from home.

Potential Pitfalls

What if you get the green light to work from home? What comes next? A lot of that will depend on a few variables. Are you blazing new ground and will be the first to work out of the office? Are you an Entrepreneur trying this for the first time? If you are the first in your company to do this, you might encounter some of the pitfalls I had when I started working from home. At the time, no one else in my office worked remotely.

The problem with being a transplant from a corporate office to a home office is that nobody quite knows how to work with you right away. If you are the first one to try this, you will need to take the initiative and put systems for success in place. When I first started in a home office, it was a really interesting practice because at the time I worked in a very small office, just 7 or 8 people. It was a lively office where we constantly ran in and out of each other's offices. It was very collaborative.

So one of the first things I did was to schedule short, catch-up meetings with key people. These 20-minute meetings were literally my replacement for water cooler chat, breakroom opportunities. I wanted to make sure that I was still actively plugging myself into the team. These meetings became an essential strategy as I developed my systems for working from home. As you consider moving to a home office, think about what that will eliminate from your day to day work life. Will you miss team collaboration, will you miss catching up with your boss over coffee? Identify these items and then look for ways to build them back in from a home office.

ORGANIZATION IS KEY FOR SUCCESS

Where will you work?

Some days I work from the couch, some from the kitchen table, but my most productive days are spent at my desk. I've worked from home for over a decade now and my office space has evolved over time. Originally, I spent my days working at a small kitchen work desk downstairs and a small roll top desk upstairs...conveniently located near the kids' toys, but neither provided the space I sometimes missed from my days in the office.

So my Pinterest-loving, DIY, crafting self decided that in the interests of my sanity and productivity I needed an office that would meet my work needs and help hide some of my inevitable paper piles from view!

At the time, my dining room was an underused hodgepodge of furniture pieces I had collected over the years. It was home to the family piano, a china cabinet and a table I got shortly after college, a curio cabinet that I will never again try to move upstairs (can you say solid wood!!), and there's also a lovely buffet piece tucked away in the corner. Everything is well used and packed to the gills, but the room itself feels cluttered, and is seldom used as anything more than a catchall or holiday overflow.

I spent some free time with a room planner for a few months to figure out what I wanted to do with the space and try to visualize how to make storage, functionality and design all components of any improvement we made. It took some time, but I managed to get some ideas on paper. It's easy to create a home office, just like it's easy to head off to an office to work. It becomes difficult when you try to merge office and dining room, work and family. I wanted something that served multiple purposes.

Over time, I have worked at that redesigned office/dining room, from a patio table in the backyard, from co-working spaces, from a condo in Florida, from my couch, from a treadmill desk and from my current craft room/office combo in our new house.

My point here is, you really can work from anywhere. If you don't have a dedicated office, don't let that hold you back. Carve out a small spot to make your own and figure out what you need to focus. Do you need to face a window, so that house chores don't distract you? Do you need to wear headphones? What helps set you up for success?

I use a combination of routines where I get rid of distracting issues like dishes in the sink and kiddie clutter, a dedicated work space, and a daily system of to-dos to keep me focused and on track. More about that later!

Schedules

Schedules, schedules schedules. If you've been around the MentoringU community for any length of time, you've likely heard me preaching the value of schedules. Some people love them and some people don't, but almost everyone understands the value of knowing what you have to do and when you have to do it.

Some people think schedules limit you and hold you back. That they create situations when you can't be flexible. I truly hope that this chapter will be an eye-opening look at how schedules or frameworks can really help you tame the chaos and stress that juggling work, family, and self can cause. Schedules put building blocks in place so you know what to expect from your days, and yet they can always change. Nothing is so set in stone that it can't be changed, but without a starting point, your day can quickly spiral into a reactionary mess.

I see schedules as a way to create opportunities for consistency, for productivity, and for peace of mind. With a schedule, you can make sure you're not missing anything important at work and at home.

You make sure that the priorities you absolutely need to get done each day are going to happen.

You can make sure that you are creating opportunity for travel, for self-care, for exercise, for work...for whatever is necessary and vital to you.

At the end of the day, having a schedule can set you up for success in ways that you can't even imagine.

When I first started working from home, I looked all over for resources to help me get organized. I'm a planner by nature and I wanted a plan. At the time, I had a 4-month old baby and was starting back to corporate work from a simple home office setup in my dining room. I knew I needed to create a schedule with time to care for the baby, do work, make phone calls, and occasionally head out to meetings in the area. The only book I could find that was anywhere near what I was looking for was written in the late 90s and didn't deal with some of the technology that had taken over in the last decade or so. Technology can be a blessing and a curse, a productivity tool and a distraction.

While the routines themselves didn't work for my purposes, the mention of a daily ritual to start and end your day did resonate with me. The book mentioned how this couple started each day at their house, sitting on the beach drinking coffee, visiting with each other and watching the waves roll in. This one hour was sacred each morning, and became a daily ritual, which was so much a part of their focus that if skipped, they felt like the day never got off to the right start.

There are tasks and symbolic processes like that for everyone. Morning rituals that we do that just balance and center us. Maybe it's your morning yoga or second cup of coffee. Maybe it's a walk with your dogs, or an audio book you listen to during a morning commute. Are you a workaholic who is out the door by 5:00am to beat traffic and enjoy a quiet office? Is your day not off to the right start unless you hit the gym or get a workout in?

Whatever it might be, we all have items that we do so often that they sometimes slip into the background. As you are working toward crafting your schedule, take a minute to use the Chasing Balance Schedule Creator interactive tool. It will help you think through these routines each day and put a framework in place.

When I'm working with a MentoringU client and we begin crafting a schedule, we start with writing it all down. This can be pen and paper, it can be a printout of an online calendar you already use, but especially for entrepreneurs, this becomes very important. Having a calendar where you are actively planning your activities, both personal and professional, and creating free and available time is essential to building a business that still allows time for your personal and family life. You might already have a work schedule, or personal calendar, but how often do they conflict? Maintaining separate calendars for work and personal is something I still do, knowing my routine helps avoid conflicts. If you are chasing work-life balance, schedules that give equal precedence to work and family priorities will help tame the chaos you might be feeling. We all have different priorities and you need to find a way to make your various priorities work together.

The first step is a deep dive on your priorities. Identifying work and life priorities is essential to creating a system or schedule that balances them successfully.

Here's a snapshot of the recent statistics about working families from the Pew Research Center study:

- *46 percent of families have two full-time working parents.*
- *17 percent of families have a full-time employed dad and a part-time employed mom.*
- *26 percent of families have a full-time employed dad with the mom serving as a stay-at-home parent.*
- *When both parents work full-time, most say that neither career takes priority.*
- *54 percent of mothers report being responsible for children's schedules and activities.*
- *47 percent of parents say they share care responsibilities when children are sick.*
- *56 percent of working parents report difficulty balancing work and family. This accounts for 60 percent of mothers and 52 percent of fathers saying it is difficult*

> - *Parents report finding more enjoyment in parenting when they have balance between work and life.*
> - *59 percent of working parents say that being a working parent has made no difference in their career advancement.*
> - *However, 41 percent of mothers and 20 percent of fathers report that being a working parent has made career advancement harder.*
> - *40 percent of full-time mothers compared to 29 percent of part-time or unemployed mothers report feeling rushed all the time.*
> - *As for spending time with their children, 50 percent of fathers and 39 percent of mothers say that they spend too little time with their children.*

What are your family priorities? What tasks or activities are you trying to balance. Which ones are easy, and which ones are you struggling with?

Some of the most common are:

- Being a good parent
- Time for self-care or exercise

- Dinner together every night
- Being present and available for family
- Reducing mealtime stress

Think through what really matters to you and what you feel like you're missing that causes you to look for balance. Do you feel like you are always rushing in the evening and can't give family the time you want to?

The next step is to define your work or career priorities.

- More balance and flexibility
- Career advancement
- Financial compensation
- Recognition in the office

The issue can become how to balance something like career advancement and better financial compensation against competing family priorities of more time spent at home, fewer working hours and less stress. Often, people think of their priorities in a silo and end up feeling overwhelmed because what they want to pursue at work is contradictory to what they want to pursue at home.

If your goals are to be there for your children and be able to be homeroom mom and be at the school volunteering, all the while maintaining your work responsibilities, then, again, you need to make sure that your work priorities are aligned. Often, this means you need to adjust your schedule to allow for the balance you are looking for. Maybe working early is a good strategy, so you're free earlier in the afternoon. Perhaps, it's a work balance with your spouse, where they work longer hours two days a week, and then you switch, so you're both planning for shorter hours on certain days and you can schedule accordingly. Whatever the right solution for you is, the idea here is to use a schedule to carve out time for work and family priorities.

I've worked with entrepreneurs who have spent years building incredibly successful businesses, only to find out that once they were successful it wasn't the vision of success that they started out looking for. They might have this incredibly successful business with employees and great financial success, but it required them to be working more than ever. If career was their only priority, this might be fine, but often, entrepreneurs want a business structure that allows for more personal and family time, not less. It's vital to build your business with that in mind so you don't create a business that perpetuates the problem you're trying to escape. This is especially important if you are building a business based on yourself as the product or brand. For example, if you are a business coach and time with you is the product, you would need to consider ways to scale your business without using more of your time. Otherwise, you are pursuing success that is solely based on the number of hours you can work directly with a client. Any reduction in the amount of time you were willing to work would likely result in a reduction in your income. That is a great example of not aligning your work priorities and your personal priorities. If you're not consistently working toward both personal and work priorities, re-evaluating as you go, then you will really get into a situation where years down the road you might be in a place where you are very successful career-wise, but still frustrated personally.

How I build my schedule

First, I start with defining my priorities. I have a simple worksheet you can download from www.chasingbalancebook.com/bonus to define your work and personal priorities. This can change, but it is usually pretty consistent year to year. I usually work through this in December as a part of my annual planning I do in the quiet week between Christmas and New Year. Something about that week just lends itself to planning for a bigger and better, and balanced new year.

Next, I work through my goals for the year. I usually have a few personal goals, like spending more time on self-care, spending less time on work, and eating dinner together every night with my family. For career, my goals focus more on the financial success I hope to achieve, new programs I hope to launch, or even a book that I am determined to see published (this book has been on my goal list for two years!).

Finally, I spend a significant chunk of time, usually around 6 hours or so, mapping out my business strategy for the year. This is important to me as an entrepreneur, since so much of the competing priorities between work and family flare up when I'm in the middle of a launch or creating a new product. If you don't create an annual plan for your business, I encourage you to check out the Social Strategy and Content Creator training and system at MentoringU (yes, this is a shameless plug for a product that makes my world just work!).

By spending time to map out what is going to happen and need to be produced each month, I'm able to better plan and be aware of when to keep our schedules as light as possible so I don't end up overwhelmed and stressed with competing priorities. If you are working from home for an employer, it might still be beneficial to look at your busy season and know that those times of year are not good for overloading personal activities.

Once I have my priorities, my goals, and my business plan, I pull up the school calendar and my calendar tool of choice to start plugging things in.

I use Google Calendar for a few reasons. One, it's free and works on any device. I always have it with me. I use it for both personal and work. And with the business version, it allows me to schedule appointment time slots so that clients are able to book time with me during blocks I've set up to be available. If you run a business that offers discovery calls, client screening calls, etc., this is essential to reducing all of the many emails being sent back and forth to try and find a convenient time for both parties to talk. My clients can view the open time slots on my business calendar and book me at the time that works for them.

I also love the ability to share calendars. I've shared my personal google calendar over to my work account and can view all my commitments, personal and work on the same screen. It allows me to respond quickly when opportunities come up, without worrying that I'm overbooking myself.

For any activity you do daily, and we'll dive into this more in the next section on daily rituals, you can schedule recurring activities on your calendar. I schedule everything, including exercise, meditation and my morning and evening daily rituals. This might seem like an overkill, but if the time is blocked off on my calendar, it helps the task to get done.

I also schedule meetings with myself each week for a few key tasks, like reviewing my financials. On a weekly basis, for me, every Friday morning at 9:00am, that's what I do. I have a window of time blocked off specifically to sit down, send invoices, follow up on estimates, and make sure that I'm treating my business like a business.

There are a few other key business tasks that I ensure are blocked on my calendar as recurring meetings with myself. As our world has increasingly become more digital, running a business has significantly changed. For one, customers expect instant gratification, from being able to order and download a product, to instant response times for concerns or feedback. We also have seen a mammoth shift in how businesses are marketing their products and services, with more and more marketing budgets being committed to social media. Entrepreneurs also express often feeling overwhelmed by social media and, therefore, often being inconsistent with it. One strategy I use to reduce that stress and leverage consistency is scheduling my social media and blog content.

I start with an annual content plan, using the tool I mentioned earlier. Then I break that down on a quarterly basis and spend one day creating massive amounts of content. Blog content, newsletter content, posts for twitter, Facebook, Instagram and Pinterest, and even ideas for YouTube videos. Then once a month I spend 2-3 hours scheduling everything I've created. This lets me leverage my upfront planning, but also have a chance to make sure the information is all still relevant and timely. Each week, I spend about 30 minutes a day posting in groups, commenting on posts, and building relationships. Without this kind of plan for content creation and posting, I would be consistently looking for content, trying to write content and posting on the fly.

The idea is to always be ahead of the game, always trying to be proactive in planning and marketing my business so it can grow, not just maintain. Scheduling a month out also ensures I'm not stressed when priorities shift and I need to shift my focus. I know that the basics are covered and I can be flexible if needed. Kids get sick, client issues can pop up, things always seem to happen, but with a plan you can tackle that calmly and with less stress when life catches up with you. The last task I have recurring on my calendar is my daily ritual to close down business each day. That includes making client follow-up phone calls and half an hour every day to run through my email and clear out anything that got overlooked during the day. I do not schedule over meetings with myself regardless of whether they are work or personal. I treat them just like I would meetings with clients, and they are one of the strategies I attribute my success to.

Getting into the nitty-gritty for just a minute... Once I've scheduled all of that on my calendar, I know when I have time available for other activities. Between scheduling my standing business meetings with myself, my open appointment slots for clients to book time with me, and having my annual marketing and promotion plan scheduled into the calendar, I have a pretty clear idea what my business weeks are going to look like. When I share my personal calendar over to my business, I can also see how that lines up with school events, days off, and major activities for the family. This bird's-eye view of my work and personal life helps me to not overbook myself and ensures I have downtime built in.

One more note on appointment time slots on your calendar. For many entrepreneurs who run a service-based business and take client calls or meetings, appointment booking can be a great way to book more engaged clients with less effort on your end. The key is to make sure you have your standing meetings booked on your calendar so that you are giving clients the flexibility to book on their schedule, but ensuring the time is convenient for you. I can't count the number of times I answered a client call when the house was quiet, only to have a baby suddenly wake up and start crying while I was on the phone. It's like they know! Over time, I have learned to book my client calls during certain windows when I can focus on the client and not spend it quietly praying the baby stays asleep.

Daily Rituals

Although much of this book focuses on the need for flexibility in your schedule, there are certain daily rituals that I stick to each and every day. My day always starts with coffee. I drink my coffee while I go through my emails deleting the junk, flagging those that need responses and creating calendar blocks for ones that are going to take more time to answer. My day always ends with making a Top 3 Things that must get done tomorrow list. These rituals are a consistent part of how I get things done.

Flexibility

Entrepreneurs who are either starting out working from home, or employees leaving the nine to five and coming to work from home, are often excited about the flexibility they see in their future. Sometimes it's enthusiasm for fitting more personal activities into their work day, like being able to meet their kids at school for lunches. For some, it's excitement about reducing the working hours because they foresee getting their work done in less time without the distractions of the office. All of this is possible, but be sure and build flexibility into your schedule and your thought process. It takes time to acclimate to a new working environment...time to balance the competing objectives on your time.

Especially in the early days, it's really important to have a solid understanding of what flexibility really means to you as an entrepreneur. If you are your own boss, and you decide you don't want to work from home today, you'd rather spend a day at the beach, what's to stop you? You absolutely could.

However, if you're trying to set yourself up for success and you're trying to find work-life balance, and some of your priorities include retiring at forty, then taking Fridays off to not work isn't aligned with the path you need to be on to achieve the success you want. This is an important concept to note for a couple of reasons. Just like a high-schooler used to schedules and restrictive environments has been known to go a little crazy once on their own at college, the employee used to a strict office-based, time-clock punching environment might become a bit resistant to schedules when they start to work from home.

Sometimes the idea of flexibility can be so enticing that we can derail our own objectives. By now it's pretty clear that I'm a big advocate of scheduling your time to maximize your efforts on your work and life priorities. We have to make sure that we are building toward our goals with our priorities in mind. When an opportunity comes along, take a minute to think about it. This might be taking on a new client, moving your business in a new direction, or maybe even a promotion or opportunity at work.

Sometimes we have to say no to something good so we can say yes to something great. It's so easy to say no to something we don't like or we don't want to do. It's not as easy to say no to something that is good and might be good for us financially. Maybe it's a high-paying client, but one that will need a lot of time devoted to them. Maybe it's a job that would be good for you, but is it taking you in the right direction? Is it heading toward the goals you want?

There is not a right answer here; just a question to give you pause when opportunities come along so that you can make an informed choice. Don't change the goal; change the plan. Be flexible in what you are implementing day to day, but be true to the goals you want to achieve.

Working from Home with Kids

My journey into working from home started when I was faced with fitting childcare into my priorities. I decided that I didn't want to miss a moment. I wanted to be at home with my child, but I had followed a fairly traditional path and had gone to a great school, got a fabulous education, and a good job. It was a little mind-boggling that now that I had achieved the success I had been working toward for years, all of a sudden something else has become a priority.

At the time I was working for a consulting firm launching environmental programs, which spoke to not only my love of logistics but also my love of the environment. I also was able to do a lot of training and education, which I was well suited for. Even now, I manage to work training and education into my business pursuits.

I grew up in childcare. My brother and I went to a daycare before and after school for most of our childhoods. I don't have any negative connotations. Instead, I remember great teachers, good friends and lots of fun on the playground. My aversion to putting my baby into childcare had more to do with my personal desire to be a full-time mom. Unfortunately, this is something that so many women face. Many of us are faced with the need to bring in an income and the desire to be at home.

Working from home was a strategy that allowed me to find balance between needing income and wanting to be at home. I did have to bring in childcare help, even with my flexible schedule. If I had been running my own business exclusively at the time, I might have been able to make it work without childcare, but I knew that I would need to go out to meetings regularly, and for that, I needed a childcare provider I trusted.

I was able to work with a part-time nanny who was able to watch my child three days a week from 8 to 1. I still got up early to work through major tasks, and I still managed my time so that the afternoons were filled with flexible tasks that were not time-sensitive. Planning was essential. In the end, it was worth the planning and juggling since I could still observe the baby playing, still be there for a quick story now and then. The nanny would put the baby to sleep before she left for the day and I usually got another 2 hours done before calling it a day.

Yes, it requires juggling and commitment to planning, but I got to be a mom and a career woman. I won't say it was easy, but it is possible. With the right strategies you can make the best of what you have to work with.

For instance, one thing that really helped me acclimate to motherhood and working from home at the same time was coming back to work slowly. I know that not everyone can plan for a longer-than-usual maternity leave, but taking ten weeks off and then phasing my work schedule back up really helped me. I started back at two hours a day for a week, then four hours a day for a week, then six hours a day for a week, and finally back up to a full-time schedule.

I used a combination of paid time off, short-term disability, and part work, part vacation. I wasn't covered by FMLA at the time, so I had to get creative with my vacation time and the other options my company offered. This combination of maternity leave and phased re-entry to the workforce really made a difference for me.

It allowed me to ease my way back up to full speed. Looking back, I am beyond grateful that I was able to do this. I was blessed with a wonderful child who I adore, but for the first nine months, I was exhausted since the baby didn't sleep well. I mean, really, really exhausted. Putting the milk in the pantry and my cell phone in the freezer exhausted. I was not at my best, and in hindsight, taking an extended maternity leave was essential for me to get back to being my normal self.

As I started back to work, especially when I was only working a few hours a day, I realized very quickly that I needed transparency for myself and my team on my schedule. It was probably the most difficult transition for me. When you start working from home and your office is always 10 feet away, it can be difficult to disconnect and officially end your day. I would hear my office phone ring, pick up the call, and end up in the middle of a two-hour issue. That's when the stress hits - when you're trying to type one-handed, with a baby on your hip, while you get dinner ready on time. Balance isn't really about how much can you juggle; it's about knowing what to juggle and what to drop.

I needed boundaries like a new mom needs coffee. I decided that I needed to eliminate temptation wherever possible. I changed my office phone to a Google Voice line and began using the straight-to-voicemail feature. Any calls coming in after my working hours didn't even make my phone ring. I no longer had to walk away and resist the temptation to handle the issue or take the call. Instead, I had restructured my environment to reduce my stress by eliminating the temptation in the first place. In all the time since, over ten years working from home, I have never had an issue so urgent it couldn't wait until the next morning. (Disclaimer: If your job deals with crises or matters that are by nature more urgent, make smart choices on your accessibility.)

It Needs to be Done Right Now…or Does It?

Sometimes we have a sense of urgency, and we feel compelled to finish things immediately. Ever been there? Working from home, this is a situation you will likely find yourself in often. It's easy to want to keep working to finish a task. When you first start working from home, shutting down and walking away from the computer will actually be a bit harder. It's important to change your mindset and know that you have time allocated to handle each task. Knowing this can reduce that urgency, because you've built a good schedule and put systems in place. You know that you don't have to answer all your follow-up emails at 5:45 pm because you spend an hour doing just that every morning. That's not to say that a true emergency will never arise, but hopefully, it will be few and far between.

Having systems in place can set you up for success. Another strategy that really helped me out when I was first juggling a newborn and working from home was making time to exercise. I needed energy to get through the day, and I needed my beautiful and somewhat cranky baby to be happy and content. Sometimes we overlook the role nature plays in relaxing babies and helping them calm down. But if you think about it, it calms most adults down too. When you think of a "happy place," a place where you can be calm and relaxed, what do you think of? The mountains? The beach? The spa? These are all places that typically invoke nature and natural elements to deliver a sense of calm and wellness.

When you have a fussy and upset baby and you step outside of the House into the backyard, there is often a noticeable difference right away in their demeanor. There is so much to see, between the sky, the birds, the trees and the colors. It really can make a big difference. Sometimes we miss how wild and chaotic things can get when we are indoors. Often, there is a television on, or people talking and making lots of noise. For children and adults, it can become overwhelming before you even notice.

Some days, when I find it hard to focus and I'm getting easily frustrated, I step outside and just take a minute. Changing my environment can make a big difference, and often is the perspective I need. When I first started working from home, learning this strategy really played a huge role in finding my balance. When the baby would start to get fussy, and I had things that I needed to get done, I would pick him up and we would both step outside and take a break. We'd pop in the stroller or we would go for a quick walk around the neighborhood. And nine times out of ten, it set the tone for a calmer afternoon. Even better, I got a little bit of exercise, which I desperately needed as a new mom. When we're so tired, sometimes we think it's counterintuitive to go workout, thinking that it will make us even more exhausted, but it really has the opposite effect. A quick walk can do wonders for an energy boost.

The last, but definitely not least, is the one strategy that is absolutely essential to my success, which is working off a short "must-do" list. We all have a to-do list that we are constantly adding tasks to. I have one of those and it can be frustrating that it's never, ever finished. When I started working from home, I had to make the minutes count. There were days, especially when I was ramping back up to a full work schedule, when I had to prioritize like a pro. I had two hours to get key items done. I couldn't waste that sorting through emails. I began filtering my 'to-do' list into a 'must-do' list. I would grab a post-it and jot down the three things I had to finish that day to consider the day successful. I limited it to three items because I wanted to triage the to-do list and ensure these were key items each day. I started with these and focused on them before doing anything else. It was this strategy more than any others that ensured that I could have a productive two-hour or four-hour day.

What Does a Typical Day Look Like?

So what does all this look like on a day-to-day basis? I get asked all the time what my schedule looks like and how I stick to it. First, there are a few things to keep in mind. I love my schedule. It gives me structure and within it, I find flexibility. If you are someone who chafes at the idea of consistency and routine, then nothing I say to you is going to change that. Know yourself, first and foremost. Second, my schedule is a template. It ensures that I have a framework to use to build my day, but again, I find flexibility within it. Don't be afraid to modify your day to handle what life throws at you! It's also important to recognize whether you are a morning person or a night owl. Do you procrastinate certain tasks? Are you easily distracted in certain environments? Again, know yourself! Don't be tempted to build a schedule for who you want to be; build it for who you are. If you are not a morning person, don't start your day at 5:00am. That is a recipe for disaster.

When we talk about chasing balance, often, what we're really looking for is time; time for the things we want to prioritize but often don't. Does any of this sound familiar?

I want to work out but something else always seem to get in the way.

I meant to plan a meal, but there just wasn't time.

I was going to pack the lunches at night, but I just didn't have the energy.

I meant to write a blog, but needed to make phone calls first.

If that's your typical day, it's time to commit to making a change. If you want to work out but something always gets in the way, what can you do to change things up? Do you need to commit to a gym, find a workout buddy, work in exercise while playing with the kids? Whatever it is, it's important to recognize that these are all competing priorities. Creating time for them is essential if you want to find balance. Otherwise, you will always be pulled in multiple directions. Having time blocked in your schedule will ensure that the choice is not whether to work out or plan a meal; it can actually be both.

My day starts with my morning routine.

Shower, Coffee, Triage.

5:00-6:30 AM - I aim to wake up around five o'clock in the morning, although that fluctuates if my kids are going through a sleep boycott. No matter how much I crave that golden hour in the morning when the house is silent and calm, five o'clock is just too early if I was up all night with the kids. Generally, I stumble out of bed after my alarm goes off for the 3rd time. I rush through a shower, get dressed, and rush downstairs for coffee. I look over my schedule for the day while I have a coffee, and then it's time to triage my day. I open the computer and immediately go through my email. I flag anything that needs immediate attention and delete any junk mail. I create tasks on my calendar for anything that needs to get done at a later time. This ensures that there is time blocked on my calendar to complete the task. This triage typically takes 20 minutes.

6:30-7:00 AM - It's time to switch to mom mode and get the kids out the door to school. I wake everyone up, pack lunches while they get dressed and ready. I set out simple breakfast and usher them through packing their backpack and getting out the door. Every day, it's a complete crapshoot on whether this goes smoothly or is an exercise in patience. \

7:15 AM - I spend about 30-45 minutes doing personal house tasks. Often, I start a load of laundry, do the morning dishes and clean the counters and do a quick clutter clean-up. I found early on that it was much harder to focus on work when the house chores were waiting to distract me. Spending a little time each morning focused on creating a clean workspace allows me to reduce the distractions for the rest of the day.

8:00 AM - I start work and jump right into the flagged emails I noted during my morning triage. I handle each of those and then move to my Top 3 list. The bulk of my morning, which is the time I'm most productive, is spent focused on the Top 3 list. I use a Pomodoro timer chrome extension to keep me on track (for an overview on how it works check out www.chasingbalancebook.com/bonus).

Pomodoro is a strategy that leverages 25-minute-focused work increments and then switches to a five-minute break. This helps me work through the tasks quickly by reducing my tendency to multi-task and then I get up and move around when there is a break. I do this 25-min work/5-min break schedule all day.

2:00 PM - Time to shift back into mom mode. This is usually the end of my workday, but sometimes I need to fit an extra hour in after picking up the kids. I do the carpool run from 2-3pm and often spend this time in the car listening to podcasts. We get home and do our afternoon routine. The kids unpack their bags, put their lunch bags away, put any papers I need to see/sign on my desk and start their homework. We knock it out early so we can have some fun. If I need to thaw something for dinner, that happens around this time. If I need to do any additional work, I do it while the kids do homework.

3:30 PM - We try to get outside, if the weather permits. Often, we head to the park, library, or the backyard. If we're heading out to play, I almost always use my Instant Pot pressure cooker to ensure dinner is ready with minimal fuss. Between the Instant Pot, a rice cooker, a slow cooker and some takeout menus, we usually have dinner covered.

6:00 PM - I do my best to have dinner ready around 6. The kids are usually screaming for food by then and the evenings are always so much easier when dinner is ready earlier. After dinner, we tidy back up, do the dishes and do another clutter clean-up. It's amazing how much kiddie toys, clothes, shoes, books, and papers make their way downstairs in the hours after school.

7:30 PM - Time for the usual bath and bed routine. We read a few stories, rock a few dance parties and turn the lights out.

8:00 PM - I live for 8-10 pm. I adore my kiddos, but 8pm is my time. Time to work on a craft, read a book, or even write a book! I usually pour a glass of wine and spend the time binging on Netflix or surfing Pinterest.

10:00 PM - I do my best to head to bed by 10. It's essential to getting up at 5 AM when the whole routine starts all over again.

While you're figuring out your daily routines and schedules, take note of what you do consistently each day. These tasks will become the base of your schedule and are the items you want to ensure you build time around, not over.

Summer Schedules

I have to admit, even with my commitment to planning and flexible schedules, I dread the end of the school year. Nothing throws off the best laid plans like bored kids underfoot. I worry about how to keep my kids busy while I work, how to keep them from destroying the house, and how to keep them from spending the whole day fighting. Working from home is a tough concept for kids to understand. Mom is home, available and should be ready to play, right?

Occasionally, I arrange for a summer camp, but some years it just doesn't work. So what ends up happening? My priorities shift again. In summertime, I know that family priorities will more often conflict with work. I know that my days will be much smoother if I take the initiative and make sure the kids have things to do to keep them busy. So home camp begins.

Home camp is really just a good routine for the kids that doesn't rely on constant access to electronics or rely on me to entertain them. The idea is to set them up with activities and opportunities to be creative kids and give me opportunities to work. One of the biggest shifts in my schedule during the summer is how I end up working in small chunks of time. In the summer, I often wake up early and work for a few hours before the kids are up and around. After a break to get them fed and onto a morning activity, I do a bit more work before a fairly long break for lunch. We often do a quick park trip or bike ride before coming back for quiet time. Quiet time is essential! It's when

I'm able to do phone calls or short meetings. We start this ritual at the beginning of the summer and I try to be as consistent as possible with it.

Our activities change with the kids' interests, but honestly, keeping a young child busy is one of the trickiest challenges. When the kids were younger, we followed a schedule that looked something like this.

Week One - Time to get in a routine. We spent this week learning the ropes and getting our daily routine down. There are usually a few tantrums during this stage, not a lot of TV and a good bit of negotiating for more screen time and playdates. We also usually try to hit up the libraries and sign up for summer reading programs. We check out books for quiet time. One of my favorite traditions that we do during the first week of summer is our Summer Bucket list. We grab a giant poster board and everyone writes down activities they want to do during the summer. It's a great reference for what they can do when the boredom starts to hit.

Week Two through Ten - We usually have a theme each week; something like campout week. You can pull all kinds of summer week themes off Pinterest. Some of my favorites are showcased on the idea board we have at www.chasingbalancebook.com/bonus. The kids really get into it, but it doesn't have to be fancy or time-consuming. In the past, for campout week, we had mini sub sandwiches made from hot dog buns, turkey, cheese, and fixings, made spritzers with juice and sprite, set up a tent in the playroom and napped in it. Afternoon snack was s'mores made in the oven.

The key to surviving the summer with kids at home is a combination of planning and keeping it simple. Like me, my kids love lists. They love structure and knowing what the day is going to look like. We have a weekly printout of what each day looks like and it helps keep them on track. Usually, the lack of patience and resulting temper tantrums that the kids have results from a vague idea of what's ahead. If I tell them we're going to watch a movie on Monday, they will start asking for the movie as soon as they wake up. However, if I have a schedule posted, similar to what they see at school, then they find it so much easier to wait patiently for the movie at 2pm because they know it's going to happen.

As a work-from-home parent, I have to be mindful of how often I ask the kids to wait while I work on something. I am often in the middle of an email, a phone call, or a task when they need me to do something. All too often, I ask for 'just a minute' or 'sure, I'll be right there' and then time marches on and half an hour passes before I take a break. Recently, my three-year-old came into my office to ask for me to get down the playdough for her. I started to ask for just a minute when she held up her hand, palm out, and said, "No just a minutes, no in a whiles, no be patients. I need you to do this right now." She said it politely and calmly, but it really hit home that she wasn't feeling like a priority.

Even during the summer, I get up around 5 am, an hour much better suited to sleeping, but it's quiet and I get through a lot of work quickly, especially since I don't have to stop to go drop the kids off at school. I get up at that ridiculously early hour to ensure that my major tasks and priorities get accomplished. I immediately head to my office and get straight to work. I start with my top three list and knock out the most important tasks first, which in my case often includes narrating trainings, something that can be next to impossible to do once the kids are up and making noise.

That led us to our first official round with more mainstream daycare. I'll be honest, I wasn't happy with it. I know a lot of people have a great experience with daycare chains, but we did not. Items went missing, staff turnover was high, too many kids in a class, and constant sickness plagued our 9-month stint. At that point, we withdrew from the daycare and returned to a smaller, church preschool setting that seems to fit our lifestyle better.

So my two cents...this is an incredibly personal decision that will have a lot to do with your priorities, your availability, and how flexible your schedule is. When you are looking at balancing working from home and caring for children, think about how you can make the priorities for both work together. Having kids at home while working is definitely more challenging, but it's possible with the right schedule or support system. If having your kids at home is a priority, it's up to you to search for the ways to make it work. In the end, whatever you choose has to be in your comfort zone.

There was a time, not too long after I started working from home, when a friend asked me for childcare advice. I honestly wasn't sure how to respond. I didn't email or text a response. I really didn't think my somewhat retro-opinion would go over very well. However, before I get to my possibly controversial opinion, let's take a walk down memory lane.

With my three kids, we've tried out quite a few options when it comes to childcare. I've juggled my kids and work myself and questioned my brilliance when things went nutty. I relied on a flexible stream of relatives, close friends, and the benevolence of my employer to make things work. I have even spent far too many hours working meetings and phone calls around nap schedules and quieter times of the day. I loved this scenario in my head, on paper, and occasionally in real life.

The problem was, as I'm sure anyone who's been around children know, kids aren't trains and you can't make them run on time. I would end up stressed, strategically pushing the mute button and simultaneously working and praying. I took a very long maternity leave with my firstborn and phased back on to work slowly. For the most part, this system worked for me until I was back full time. At that point I realized I needed more help.

That's when Madison entered our lives. She was a nanny who I adored...until she left us to go to law school, that is. Just kidding, we still adore her!

For a year and a half, she was a huge part of our lives and made the sunshine just a little bit brighter. I could still work at home and hear my son's baby laughs and giggles. I could poke my head around the corner and see him decorating the kitchen in pureed sweet potatoes. Most of all, I didn't feel like I was missing anything. I knew he was well cared for and happy because I was nearby to watch.

One of the biggest struggles for any new parent is trusting those they've entrusted with their children. I knew I would have to continue working once I had children, and I quickly realized this was going to be one of the hardest parts of early parenthood for me. Hiring help was a big step. I realized that I couldn't do it all on my own, and that I needed to prioritize working from home with kids by finding a solution. Madison not only helped my son learn and grow in the first years, she also helped me trust caretakers with him later on.

When we hired our nanny, we knew she was in college and there was a finite amount of time she would be available to us. Attending her graduation luncheon was bittersweet. By then we had grown to know her, we wanted the best for her, and I knew she would make a darn fine lawyer one day. It was also the end of an era for us, though, since I knew we would have to make other arrangements for my son. For a few weeks, I tried to manage things on my own, but it didn't last long. It lasted just long enough for me to remember that there was a darn good reason I had hired help in the first place.

Thus started the era of the small neighborhood church preschool, which was great but expensive. That was a bit of an adjustment for us. Arriving and picking up at scheduled times, my son had to adjust to other napping conditions and, of course, the onset of separation anxiety. We also hit the school during a sudden onset of staff turnover, which left me very uncomfortable at the beginning. Once things leveled out, I was happy with the location, teachers and my son's adjustment, but man, the beginning was rough. Time went on and he grew and before I knew it he was in preschool. Same school, so no sudden transition there and I absolutely loved his teacher. When she left to start her own in-home childcare and focus on kinder prep, we followed her without a thought.

Our in-home experience was fabulous, but owe most of that to knowing my provider beforehand in a school setting. I was her classroom parent and spent a lot of time with her one on one. She also kept her class size small, only 5 kids were in her kinder prep in-home care. They had Spanish, music and art teachers, and during the day, she taught them core curriculum for kinder that prepared my son well for his first year. My son also had the chance to learn in a way that we don't teach anymore. My provider's husband did several projects with the kids during the school year, from building forts in the play area to working with them on birdhouses, demonstrating life skill lessons that aren't always a part of school teaching. We loved it!

But time continued marching on and soon my son was ready for kindergarten and my daughter's nanny had graduated, leaving us in a position of new childcare situations for both kids.

Volunteering...The Third Job

Sometimes I wonder if I would try to balance as much if I worked in the office. Something about working from home and being instantly able to shift from Working Woman to Multitasking Mom on a moment's notice makes me more inclined to commit to after-school activities and planning teacher luncheons...aka being a parent volunteer.

"I work from home, have a flexible schedule and want to be involved in my kids' education...I should volunteer," said a naive first-time mom. Well, I wasn't naive for long. I quickly realized that volunteering is the third job for many working parents. When my oldest started elementary school, I didn't think twice about joining the Parent Teacher Organization and volunteering my time for events and fundraising. We had started off at one charter school, but quickly realized it wasn't a good fit for us. They had just introduced their elementary program and it was a bit chaotic, as they got things figured out.

We were only there for a brief time, but not knowing that, I reached out to the PTO about helping out. I could not have been more shocked when I received a call telling me that they could interview me a few days later if I could stop by before pickup! WHAT? An interview for an organization where I'm donating my time and money? I honestly thought it was going to be a meet and greet, and the interview was just terminology. Nope, it was an honest to goodness interview. There were three ladies across the table from me, firing off questions of what I would do in various situations, how I would handle certain projects, and how many hours I could guarantee. The only saving grace to that crazy hour long interview was when they asked me what I drank because margaritas are a must to hang with them. This volunteering was a whole new world!

When my son switched schools two months later, with the school year already underway, I knew I was going to have to make an effort to get plugged in and involved at his new school. I wasn't sure about trying the PTO route again, but luckily enough, I literally stumbled into some amazing women the day I first dropped him off. Little did I know that I had run into the very group that was at the core of anything and everything that happened at our new school. This group of women were amazing and I knew that friendships were in the making! I told them laughingly that I loved to help out and they hadn't seen the last of me.

A few weeks later, I attended my first PTO meeting, where I heard some complaints voiced about the lack of communication from the school and PTO that was leaving parents with questions but no recourse for answers. I offered to jump in where another parent had left off and create the PTO website. Funny enough, no interview was needed! A few meetings later, I was knee-deep in volunteering at the school.

Then came my personal Waterloo! International Fest...an amazing event intended to open the eyes and minds of children and teachers at our school and allow them to embrace the diversity and culture that our charter school represented. My planning expertise landed me the position of a logistics coordinator, and I had no idea what I was in for. For over four months, I participated in conference calls, meetings, craft sessions, shopping trips, video production, promotions creation, and teacher education! Looking back, it was truly an amazing event, but it definitely raised a big question for me.

To Volunteer or Not to Volunteer...it's an eternal question. When you volunteer, your efforts benefit your child and others, the school itself, the teachers and other parents. Your time is given over to benefit the collective, but what does that do on a small-scale to your family.

While I know that volunteering does benefit my children, does he?

For my young children, the activities I do for them, for their school, their class, their teams…I do them all with my children in mind, but in their eyes, it's just one more thing (more realistically a dozen more things) Mom has to do before she can play.

I've added volunteering to my list of jobs. It gets analyzed when I'm making priority lists, and it factors into my goal setting and scheduling. First and foremost, I'm a Mom; it takes priority over everything else. Second, I'm an employee of a great company and work set hours to get that work done. That means I need to be strategic about volunteering, something I feel is important for me to do as a person and as an example to set for my kids. It also means that I need to weigh that time commitment against my family priorities of spending more time being with my kids. Running less and playing more. It's all about finding that balance!

Working from Home with a Spouse

Just before 2012 went out in style (and escaped the dreaded Mayan end of the world apocalypse...remember that?), my husband took a new job. We were both very happy with this move. It was very rewarding professionally, looked like a great fit both travel wise and financially, and it was a home-based position when he wasn't on the road. I'm very passionate about telecommuting and was excited to share this with him.

Remember that story about the couple that got up and drank coffee together while figuring out their day? Yep, I had visions of that blissful scenario running through my head. I did not factor in the three ring circus that occurs each morning when I'm trying to get everyone out the door and off to school.

When I began to mention to people that he would be working from home alongside me, I received a lot of unsolicited opinions and advice. There were the "Oh no" group who gasped wondering how we were going to get anything done for our respective positions. They assumed we would both be too distracted to work. There was the "that's awesome, now he can take the kids to school" group who, like me, immediately saw how our parenting workload might shift. And there was the "I'd never get anything done" group, who probably aren't cut out to be telecommuters anyway.

From the start, it's been great, but there were definitely a few things that were key to our success in both working from home.

One, we knew we would each need our own space. Several months back, we remade our dining room over into my office (in a way that still allowed the room to serve its purpose during entertaining events). Check out the design and before and after pictures! Since my space was located downstairs, we (a.k.a, me) determined that his "office" was going to have to fit into either the upstairs family room or our bedroom. Since my husband travels a good deal, I wanted his office to be able to disappear when he was on the road.

A few quick Pinterest searches later and I was on the hunt for an Armoire Style desks. I would be able to shut the doors and it would be bye bye office, hello bedroom every day at 5.

I happened to be in an awesome thrift store about three days later, and couldn't believe it when I spotted one! It was in good shape, and even had an L-table drop down for extra office space. I was good and waited semi-patiently until he returned from that week's travel. I didn't even give him time to unpack properly before I dragged him off to the store to take a look. Bada bing, bada bam…Hubs had a new office. All went well until we got it home and had to get it upstairs. Remember that scene from Friends where Ross shouts pivot at Rachel and Chandler taking the couch upstairs... it was something like that with the heaviest piece of furniture I could imagine. It's the reason we hired movers when we eventually moved out of that house! We did finally get it upstairs, and after a few days, I think I was forgiven for finding and buying the heaviest piece of furniture ever made. I'll be the first to admit my spacious office setup that took over the entire dining room, and my husband's 'office in a box' armoire are not equal, but it works. We each have our own space, own office supplies, own phone lines, own printers, etc. Best of all, we can meet up for lunch every day!

Another thing we learned early in that co-telecommuting phase was that office hours are a must. I learned this one the hard way years ago when I first began working from home. I needed to shut the computer, switch off the work cell phone and walk away from work just as I had when I would physically leave an office. It is way too easy to walk by a computer, see email sitting in your inbox and lose an hour on something that would have just as easily been tackled the next morning. I'm a minority in my company since I still haven't synced up my phone with the email servers and don't work on weekends and vacations, but it helps me keep the balance between work and life. This is something my husband, who at the time was new to telecommuting, had to really work on, and continues to struggle with. I'll occasionally search the house for him and find him hiding in his armoire checking just one more thing for work.

It will also be important that you find a routine that works for you. I work early in the morning, take a break to get the kids ready and off to school, and then finish up in time to pick them up. Fitting in daily exercise is something I struggle with. Outside of that, my routine really allows me to focus on where I truly want to be, when I want to be there, which in my case is being available for my kids when they get home from school. With my husband joining me in telecommuting, we've been able to improve on our routine, splitting up who takes and picks up each kid to allow both of us to spend some one on one time with each kid each day.

This one will vary by person, but for me, I need a coffee frother, the gym, and Pandora. I know those don't make a lick of sense in the same sentence, but they are all vital to making telecommuting work for me. I'm a coffee fanatic and a loyal Starbucks customer through and through. Although I still hit up my favorite local coffee shop on Fridays, most of the time it would mean a special trip out, out of my way, just for coffee. What's the point in sitting in traffic for coffee when you telecommute? I stumbled on a coffee frother one day and haven't looked back since! Each morning, I mix up my own latte at home and Starbucks has become more of a treat than a daily vice. The gym is my husband's escape. At the end of a day working from home, eating at home and not leaving, other than to pick up the kids, he escapes to the neighborhood gym for a workout and some socialization. Last but not least, Pandora = Productivity for me. A good jamming playlist, a quiet house and a long to-do list that gets knocked out quickly is a daily ritual for me.

Calendar blocks are also essential. When I have tasks to do that are not meetings with others or travel, I schedule them as meetings on my own calendar. This is one of the first tips I give to anyone new to working from home. For instance, if I need to create social media messages, work on my to-do list, send a block of emails or draft a presentation, I make it a point to put a block of time on my calendar, marked as busy, to work on those objectives. The hardest part for my peers when I moved to working from home was not having the visual that I was busy. I ended up with a lot of random, last-minute requests that kept me from completing my tasks. Scheduling my tasks on my calendar gave them clarity on my schedule and kept me on task.

Using Tools and Tech to Find Your Balance

Get what you need. There are lots of great tools out there, enough that you could spend more time exploring than using them. Be sure you look for tools that meet a need you have. Anything else, bookmark or pin for future reference, but don't waste time on it until you need it.

Read Reviews. Always read reviews for current and past versions before opting in for a tool. Whether you pay for the tool, or it's free, you are investing your time in learning how to use it, creating within it, and you need to ensure it's a valid product that isn't going to frustrate you by being buggy and sluggish.

Use the tutorials. Are you the type that jump into a new tool, program or software, ignore the tutorial and think you can figure it out? Why waste your time? Most apps, software, and programs have a tutorial that is shown the minute you login. Spend time to watch the short tutorials and learn. Reducing the learning curve on the frontend can save you so much time later on...that it is truly time well spent.

Always check the different versions available. Many times, the developers of the great tools do a great job with showing you the benefits of the more expensive version of their tool. That doesn't always mean it's the best version for you. I often start with the free version and upgrade when I outgrow it. It helps me get a feel of the user interface, how the tool works, and if it's actually going to do what I need it to. A few times, a free or demo version wasn't available and I ended up burned by a tricky software with a steep learning curve. A free or demo version would have quickly shown me that it wasn't a good fit for me and I would have changed my mind about my purchase.

Pay for the tools that are worth it. Some tools have a cost and are worth the payment. I pay for video editing software on my iPhone that creates awesome short movies and removes the app logo at the end. With the software, I can create movies during meetings, or events, and upload them to YouTube before I even head home. The convenience and how often I use the tool makes the cost worth it for me.

Keep a bookmark folder, or use a launch tool like Toby or Start.me for easy reference. There is nothing worse than knowing you have seen the perfect tool, and you can't find it again. I have a bookmark folder specific to productivity tools, editing tools, etc., and I save things that catch my attention immediately. I use tools like Toby to organize the tools by tasks. So if I'm working on a blog post, I might have a selection of tools that have to do with headline generators, research topics, etc.

For consistency in branding, use the same avatar or logo on every tool. Creating an online brand is important for any business. Be sure you are consistently creating profile information and using the same logo or avatar to ensure consistency. If you don't run a business, have fun with it and use a unique avatar!

Export final versions. If a tool gives you the option to export a final copy of what you have created, take it. There have been some great tools that I loved, and just like a great show that doesn't last the first season, the tool went quietly into the night. I lost anything that had not been exported and saved offline. It has made me something of a digital packrat!

Link with Google Drive, Dropbox, or Box, if possible. If the tool has an API or link connection to a cloud-based storage, link up and save your information over to it. Setup folders, be organized and consistent in how you name items for easy reference later on.

Most importantly, use them! Tools are only helpful if you actually use them. Only purchase or sign up for what you need, but make sure if you take the time to set up an account, create a profile, and take a tutorial, that you actually follow through and use the tool!

There are several tools that I use to make working from home productive. At www.chasingbalancebook.com/bonus, there is a complete list of these resources for you to check out and download in the bonus section.

Most of the productivity tools that I use in my business are free of charge or low cost. Not because I mind spending money on business infrastructure, especially the tools that help me get work done, but because there are some amazing tools out there that just don't cost much. I also started my business helping entrepreneurs who don't have big pools of money, and I learned a lot about what you can do with a shoestring budget. In many cases, I recommend you start with the free or low-cost tools and upgrade as you need to larger or more expensive versions. Finances can cause stress in business and at home, and Chasing Balance is about less stress, not more.

My background is in training and education, and I have spent the last decade training various audiences on different types of products. I have found that helping others solve problems using efficiency and productivity strategies is my zone of genius. It's an area that I really enjoy and am naturally drawn to.

I have always enjoyed teaching others. Growing up, I was called a know-it-all, and warned more times than I can count that it wasn't an attractive quality. I think a lot of this stemmed from being an avid reader and being exposed to so many ideas, concepts and thought processes at a young age. I often questioned how things were done, and even as a child would re-arrange, re-organize and re-structure things to try and make them better. I also learned early on that one person's idea of "better" is not always what others around you would consider an improvement. There is always someone that you can learn from if you are open to the knowledge.

As I began my journey into entrepreneurship and telecommuting, I realized this also applied. There is always an improvement that can be made to make our business work better and more efficiently, just like a new focus on meal planning or a new routine at home can make our personal life flow better. I train all different types of audiences on everything, from being comfortable on video to marketing workflows to project management, and through it all, the one thing I focus on is efficiencies.

I am a natural advocate for sharing what I know, and I believe in a collaborative, not competitive, environment. I love to research solutions and try them out. My grandmother used to say, "Not everything that glitters is gold" and I think of that all the time when a new tool or a special offer comes along. As a marketer, I see a lot of focus being put on

FOMO - the fear of missing out. It's the reason we rush out on Black Friday, grab the Amazon lightening deals, and are willing to buy something we don't need right now just in case it's not available in the future. The problem with this is that we end up spending more money and more time learning new tools without any process or filter that helps us know if it's the solution we are searching for. Tools should solve a problem. If you aren't up against an issue, you might not need the solution, even if it's a steal of a deal.

That being said, here are some of my favorite tools and the reasons that I use them.

Google Drive

An essential element to organizing my business is Google Drive. Google Drive includes Google Docs, Google Sheets, Google Slides and Google Forms, plus a drive structure where all your documents and files are stored. As a telecommuter and entrepreneur, I work a laptop lifestyle. That means that while I do work from a home office most days, I can, at any time, relocate to a coffee shop, the beach, or even a different city if we are traveling for some reason. The last thing I want to do is drag a bag full of external drives around to make sure I have all the data and documents I need. With my information stored in Google Drive, it's accessible at any time, from anywhere and from any computer. I don't worry about a hard drive crash causing weeks of lost work anymore!

There are several tutorials on Google Drive in the MentoringU Skills Lab for Entrepreneurs if you want detailed overviews, but I do want to highlight a few of the ways I use Google Drive in my business and personal life to stay organized and on top of everything from meal planning to organizing volunteer activities.

#1 - Google Forms -> Google Sheets.

Google Forms is an awesome tool for entrepreneurs, and really anyone. It allows you to build a form that asks questions and feeds those data points into a Google Sheets spreadsheet. I have used this to process interest from entrepreneurs who want to be featured in the EntrepreDOERs e-zine, collect information from classmates to build a directory for our class, collected information from teachers to create a database for parents of the teachers' favorite items, created a contract to be acknowledged and signed before work could begin for website development projects. The possibilities are endless. You can embed video and pictures and it has the ability to use logic to customize the form. Logic means if you answer question one with answer A, it takes you to page 2, but if you answer with answer B it takes you to page 3, which is very useful if you need to ask different questions based on the answers someone has already given. I've even used Google Forms as an affordable simplistic landing page when needed.

#2 - Google Sheets

Google Sheets is a robust online spreadsheet program that is similar to Microsoft Excel. I use it extensively in business since clients can prep information for migrations or other needs and then grant me access. There is no data lost or version issues that can occur when emailing spreadsheets back and forth. We have one version that we can work on collaboratively. You can even work on the same spreadsheet at the same time which is great for remote teams working together.

#3 - Google Docs

I used Google Docs to write this book. It's an online program similar to Microsoft Word and my absolute favorite feature is the ability to use Voice Typing. I can create massive amounts of content very quickly on my computer or my phone by using Voice Typing. I speak faster than I write and I find the flow is much more natural when I'm speaking. I also find it easier to get clients to begin blogging if I have them just talk to the computer about the topic. We can clean up a rambling post far faster than we can struggle through getting words on paper in many cases.

#4 Google Slides

Google Slides is a robust presentation software. It doesn't have all the bells and whistles of Microsoft PowerPoint, but it is a great, free, online alternative. I often import templates that I make or buy and they work perfectly in Slides. I use Slides for almost all of my webinars that I run. I can build in Slides, go into presenter mode and create a recording very easily. It also means that I can tweak or touch up the presentation anytime from any computer since everything, even the software, is web-based.

Gmail

I use two email programs, Active Campaign for business email marketing, and Gmail for personal and direct business email correspondence. I use Gmail as my email system of choice for several reasons.

It's a free product to get started, which is often very important as a new business or someone working from home paying for services. If you decide you want to upgrade to the business side of Google, which is what I've done for my business, it's a very affordable option, usually starting around $5/user per month.

The biggest benefits of Google Apps for Business is a larger storage drive on Google Drive, dedicated business email powered by google, and a calendar where clients can book appointment time slots. There are lots of other bells and whistles, but those are the three that I find benefit entrepreneurs the most.

The email is a big one. Perception is key when you are starting your business, and an email that ends in gmail.com (mentoringu@gmail.com) will always be seen as less professional. With Google Apps for Business, you can use your domain email (hello@mentoringu.org) for a more professional appearing email that still runs through the gmail program. You still login to gmail to check and send messages, which makes it convenient and comfortable for those just getting started.

I also love that there are several add-on applications that really take Gmail to a whole new level of productivity. You can find many of these in the Chrome Web Store, or check out our book bonuses section for an easy reference list. (www.chasingbalancebook.com/bonus)

Sidekick by Hubspot

Sidekick is a really great application that easily installs as an extension in Chrome. It creates a sidebar in your gmail that pulls up relevant social media information on the person you are writing to if you are connected on social media. It will quickly give a snapshot of recent social media activity for that person, allowing you to personalize your communications. There is also a similar extension called Sales Navigator Lite if you would rather pull LinkedIn information.

Boomerang for Gmail

Boomerang is another extension I use daily and really like. Following up is key for entrepreneurs, but we're busy folks and often end up forgetting to email or follow up for some time. This can cost you sales, clients, and deals.

Boomerang allows you to schedule follow-ups while you're drafting your original email. If I know that I need to follow up with this person in two days if they haven't responded, I can set a follow-up reminder based on a few different criteria. I can follow up if they haven't responded, if they haven't opened the email, or if they haven't clicked something in the email.

This is a great tool to help focus your efforts. If you need someone to open an attachment and review the draft, you can set up a boomerang to ensure that happens in a timely manner. Boomerang brings the email back to the top of your inbox if the recipient didn't meet the criteria you set so that you can reach back out and bring it back to their attention.

Sendtu for Gmail

Sendtu is just amazing for anyone who sends similar-style emails frequently. Templates are an essential part of any entrepreneur's arsenal, but I also think they can be life-changing for personal use. Sendtu lets you send HTML-styled emails straight from gmail. So if you are a room parent, or volunteer coordinator from school trying to catch parents' attention for an event or cause, these can be great! It's also a great tool for new businesses that want a professional look to their emails but aren't ready to make the commitment to an email marketing system. They are eye-catching and can have calls to action like RSVP, or Get Tickets Now, without having to upgrade your email platform. Check out our Book Bonuses to see these in action for personal, volunteering, and business uses. (www.chasingbalancebook.com/bonus)

Financial Tools

Let's talk finances. Whether you are working from home as an employee or are an entrepreneur working a laptop lifestyle, there are financial tasks you should have on your radar. Let me pause for just a second and say, this is not tax advice and you should take this in the spirit it is intended...as productivity and efficiency guidance from one person on a work from home journey to another. That being said, on to the good stuff...

Finances matter. I repeat, finances matter. I can't count the number of times a client has glossed over the financial conversation because of any of the following reasons:

- I just want to help other people
- I love what I do and would do it whether I was paid or not

- If I focus on providing great service, the money will follow
- It's not all about the money

While I agree with each of these statements and the passion they represent, I'm here to tell you that the money does matter. We can't aspire to success and feel guilty for following the money at the same time. There are, without a doubt, different ways to define success. There is financial success, success of achieving goals, success in following your passions. Success can be defined in many ways, but from a business perspective, it is most often defined by the finances.

Did your business make money? Did it break even? Are you in the red?

I would even go so far as to say that without a focus on the finances and what financial success means to your business, you should consider yourself a hobbyist. There is nothing wrong with being a hobbyist. My photography is a hobby. I make some money, and it pays for photography equipment I love to buy. I take classes to get better, I have a Facebook page and a website, and all the trappings of a business, but when it comes to finances, I operate it in the red. I don't mind if I spend more money than I make because my goal isn't financial success. My goal is to get out with my camera and take gorgeous pictures that fulfill a creative need for me. I spend more money on equipment and my time than I make each year, but I do this knowing that this is a hobby and because of that, I don't expect it to be profitable.

My business, MentoringU is very different. I track my financials closely. I have sales goals for each product and I check in each week to make sure they are on track. I treat it like a business, even though I am passionate about everything I do within it. At the end of each month, each quarter and each year, I expect to have income and expenses, and overall, profit. That's the difference in a hobby and a business...the consistent pursuit of profit. I make no apologies about the price of my services, my products, because I have invested time, energy and money into developing them and I am selling them just like any other business. And just like any other business, I track and monitor my finances and adjust my efforts to ensure a healthy profit.

One of the hardest parts of entrepreneurship, especially if you have turned your passion into a business, is recognizing what does and doesn't make a profit. Letting go of an idea or product if it's not bringing in business can feel traumatic.

You take an idea from conceptualization to development, to implementation to market and you wait for everyone to rush to buy it. If you laid the groundwork correctly, hopefully they are knocking down your doors. But not every product is a hit. Recognizing what does and doesn't make you money is essential for entrepreneurs. You have to focus your efforts and resources on what has profit potential, and to do that, you need to know your finances inside and out.

I use a few different tools to track my finances and my products. These are tools I spend time with regularly and they ensure that I know exactly how my business is performing at all times.

You can't grow what you don't know.

If you don't know how a product is performing, you can't fix, change, or modify it for better success.

Wave Apps

Like many of the tools I have mentioned in this book, WaveApps is a free tool. I tried several financial monitoring dashboards, pen and paper and even tried to build my own budget spreadsheet to track my finances in the beginning. The trouble was that I leveraged so many sites and tools to sell and distribute my products that it became inefficient and time consuming to check on everything. I felt like I spent an entire day each week trying to catch up on the money trail.

As time went on and my business grew, this got more and more cumbersome. I started out offering one-on-one strategy services for small businesses. I would sit down and discuss their current operations, look for inefficiencies and help them figure out the solution to fix it. That was pretty easy to track. I was invoicing via PayPal and could check a report pretty quickly to see where I was.

Then as I continue to see the same issues pop up again and again, I began to develop online trainings for some of the most common problems. I soon had courses live on Udemy, my own website, and had a Thinkific site dedicated to training entrepreneurs on tech solutions for their inefficiencies. Udemy paid out via PayPal, my website direct deposited into my business bank account, and Thinkific processed payment via Stripe.

Fast forward a few years and I added an Etsy store full of downloadable templates, I was selling my MentoringU planner systems on Amazon and various online booksellers, I had launched a membership site for Entrepreneurs looking to boost their tech skills and learn automation strategies, and I did website design, email system migration and customer database solutions for clients, all of which had various payment processing setups.

Along the way, in my research for an article on the best tech solutions for new entrepreneurs, I came across Wave. I research a lot of tools and tech to give advice to my clients, and Wave immediately caught my eye.

It was a business financial dashboard with everything I was looking for. It connected to all my payment processing gateways so that I could see all incoming income on one screen, I could pay bills out of it, I could invoice clients and even set up recurring charges for client retainer fees.

Wave keeps a running tally of my income and my expenses, allows me to categorize the multiple income streams, creates the reports I need to give to a bookkeeper at tax time, and ensures I get paid on time with automated reminders and credit card processing.

With my focus on efficiency and ensuring financial success, Wave was a perfect fit. I could quickly manage all income streams, identify what products were performing well and focus my efforts in growing them rapidly.

Regardless of what platform, program, or tools you use to track your finances, make sure you are devoting time on a regular basis to ensuring your business is heading in the right direction financially. I recommend putting a standing meeting with yourself on your calendar each week, or each month, and using that time to check in on your products and evaluate your finances. Remember, you can't grow what you don't know, so be sure you know what your money is doing!

Canva

Another tool I couldn't run my business without, and use frequently for personal projects as well, is Canva. I use Canva for anything I need to design, from my planners to fundraiser graphics for the PTO. Canva is an online graphic design software that is very easy to use and has a free account with a lot of great options.

Canva has templates for all sorts of items that you might need to create, from social media page covers to post templates, to flyers and email headers. There are invitation templates and flyers, and too many other styles to list. I use Canva daily and created the EntrepreDOERs e-zine in it, created every one of the schools Read-A-Thon graphics, sponsor letters, and social media posts in it. Check out our book bonuses section for some of the free videos I have covering how to use Canva for graphic design needs in your business.

Canva does a few things really well. One, Canva provides templates for all the most common graphic design needs for entrepreneurs so you can spend your time creating something awesome and not worrying about sizing, dimensions and file sizes. I am a huge fan of templates because they help jumpstart your productivity. Instead of spending a lot of time figuring out design elements, you can jump to adding content, updating colors, and getting something out the door. Money is made when you go to market.

Up to that point, everything is unpaid, behind-the-scenes work. Our goal is to get to market in a more efficient way and Canva can definitely help for those who struggle with creating social media content and blog graphics.

Even better, Canva provides an extensive library of images, graphics, clip art and illustrations for free, and an additional library of graphics and elements that cost $1. If you have spent any time looking at stock photography and elements, you will immediately understand the value here. Also, if you are working on a campaign and you will need a webinar presentation, social media marketing graphics for Facebook, Instagram, Twitter and Pinterest, and an email header to market your campaign, Canva makes it easy to create a design and then replicate and resize it appropriately for every platform. This is a paid option, but if you're using this for business, I highly recommend it.

Another element I love is their branding options. Whether you are using this for personal use and you want to feature your favorite colors, or using it for business and need to be true to your branding, Canva features a brand wizard. You can identify your brand colors and your accent colors, as well as fonts and text sizes. You basically create a style guide, something every business should have. Once you have created a brand style in Canva, it's automatically applied when you create a graphic. This is huge! If you are frequently creating Instagram graphics, this alone will save you so much time and ensure your branding is consistent.

Marketing Content Wizard

I start each year with an annual marketing plan. I grab a few hours, head to a coffee shop, and map out what I want to see happen that year. I have a mind map that I built years ago, and continue to add to, that features every product I've created and service that I offer. I bring that and look to see what will work for the upcoming year. The goal here is not to spend days and days planning. The goal is to leverage your resources wisely.

Often, we get so caught up in creation mode that we never get out of it. We are always building something new instead of focusing on promoting what already exists. Sometimes, this is because creating is a more solitary effort and that is our comfort zone, whereas sales is much more extroverted. As we talked about earlier in the book, know yourself. Know your weaknesses and your strengths. Outsource areas you can't or won't dive into that affect your success.

I know that I get caught up in creating new products and developing new ideas. The Marketing Content Wizard was born out of my need to focus my efforts on marketing what I had already built. I spend a few hours, four max, planning my themes, promotions, challenges, freebies and lead magnets for the year. I put rough sales goals on each of them, so I have something to measure my progress against year to year.

Then I focus on the upcoming quarter. I am an avid fan of batching work for productivity. I sit down once a quarter and map out all 12 blog posts, and rough out much of my social media and video content. The Marketing Content Wizard helps me keep this on track and on point with my goals, themes, and promotions for the month. This way, I don't end up on a soap box ranting about planning when my product and promotion for the month is something entirely different.

I always start with my blog posts. They are the hardest item to make myself write. I use Google Docs voice typing to help. It lets me talk about a topic instead of writing about it, and for me, that makes a huge difference in how quickly I can get it done. Writing all twelve blog posts usually takes me 2-3 hours. Since I focus on one theme a month and all of my topics have to do with that theme, it's usually pretty easy once I get going. Once I know my blog posts for the month, I can use that text to tease out social media posts and status updates. I usually spend about 1-2 hours per month that I'm working on, so 3-6 for the quarter, to develop the status updates and posts. Are you seeing a pattern here?

The Marketing Content Wizard template keeps me focused on my goals for the month and makes sure I'm staying on point. You can do this yourself as well; just be mindful to stay on target!

The next step is to create graphics that align with all my posts. Since I've already written my blog posts, and drafted my social media status updates, it becomes easy to see what graphics I'll need to go along with it. I log into Canva and create them all in a single sitting. This usually takes another 1-3 hours depending on how focused I am.

At this point, I've usually spent 12 hours over the course of 2-3 days, and I've created my social media posts, blog posts for the next 12 weeks. That averages out to an hour per week, and it's only possible because I batch the work. I've used this example for entrepreneurs creating marketing content, but batching is useful in so many situations. Whether you are meal planning, travel planning, or writing business newsletters, batching is a tool that can help you get in the development and productivity zone and accomplish so much in a short time.

Scheduling

Once you've built your content, the next step is to leverage the power of automation and scheduling to get your marketing out there. Businesses make money when you go to market with your product or service. If you have built an annual plan with promotions and goals, and you wrote content to market it, scheduling that content is the equivalent of pushing the Go button. It's also a step that becomes a roadblock for so many entrepreneurs. This is when the second thoughts and perfectionism creep in and slow you down. You start to re-think and re-work things. You might decide you can't publish a blog post yet because you were going to update your website first. If you want to, you can always find an excuse.

Scheduling can put your marketing on auto and take your procrastination out of the equation, especially when it comes to blogging. Blogging is a great way to increase your search engine ranking. Every blog post creates a new page on your website and gives search engines another chance to match your information with what someone is searching. If you have a basic website with a home page, services page, contact us page, freebies page, and photo gallery, that's 5 chances for Google to look at your content and think you're a relevant answer. If you blog weekly for a year, you add 52 additional website pages full of business and product-relevant content. That opens up so many more opportunities for you to gather organic traffic. If you spend the time to create the content, take the last lap and schedule it!

There is a plethora of tools for scheduling marketing content, so I'll just feature a few of my favorites.

Buffer or ViralTag

Buffer and ViralTag are both robust social media scheduling tools. I use ViralTag in my business and love some of the options, like curated content that might be relevant to my audience and the ability to schedule some of my most popular posts as evergreen content. Evergreen content is timeless content that can be re-posted at a later date. I have several of these types of posts and use them to fill in when my feed is less busy than usual.

Both Buffer and ViralTag, and most other social media schedulers, connect with your social media accounts and allow you to paste in your text and graphics and choose which channels they will be posted on. You can change this for each post, so if something isn't relevant to your twitter audience you aren't forced to post it there. You can also set up custom posting schedules so your content is posted at the most relevant times for your audience, helping to maximize your exposure.

These platforms can also be used for volunteer or personal causes when you are posting deliberate messages that were determined ahead of time. When I ran a school fundraiser, these were key to getting our message out on time. It was also very helpful because it forced us, as a group, to pre-plan our messaging and be proactive instead of reactive. Fundraising and volunteer work can often be stressful because of the last-minute feeling for many of the requests and actions needed. Leveraging some planning and organization tools can help reduce that stress and make the whole experience more pleasant.

Grum

Grum is the only Instagram scheduler I have found that lets me automate my Instagram posts. Most other Instagram schedulers send reminders to post and still make you open the app and work on it in real time. They are helpful, but they don't take the activity completely off your plate. Grum allows you to upload up to 30 graphics at a time, caption them, and add the first comment, which is very useful for adding longer strings of hashtags. You can then schedule the posts for a future time and date and they post automatically. This is especially wonderful if you are running a challenge via Instagram. I ran a 90-day productivity challenge last year and was able to schedule the entire thing. I batched all graphics in Canva, then loaded them in batches to Grum and set one to post each day. It allowed me to run the challenge and spend my time responding to comments and engaging my fans instead of posting day by day. It was a much better use of my time, day to day.

Facebook Scheduler

Facebook has a scheduling tool built into Facebook pages and groups. While you can use a third party scheduling tool like Buffer or ViralTag, Facebook prioritizes posts that are made on their site, through their tools. Everyone has priorities and Facebook has been clear about theirs! Posts scheduled through third party apps are not ranked as highly as those created using Facebook's scheduling tool. Although it is an additional step, I recommend logging into Facebook and batch-creating all your Facebook posts. You can enter your text, load your pictures or videos, pepper your content with emojis and even tag relevant fans or businesses. Then set the time and date for your post to go live and move on to the next one.

One thing to note is, if you are using Facebook's scheduler for Facebook posts, be sure not to schedule those same posts through a third party app or you'll end up posting all your updates twice.

WordPress Scheduler

WordPress is my website platform of choice for a lot of reasons, but one is definitely the blogging elements. WordPress makes it very easy to draft and schedule blog posts ahead of time. If you've used the Content Creator Wizard, you can just cut and paste your content. If you haven't drafted your content, you can login and draft it directly into WordPress. When you have your content in place, you can load images or videos. This is very important if your user base is also a good target audience for Pinterest. Pinterest relies on "pinnable" content and you have to have images or videos in your post to pin. Leverage Canva to create these quickly and efficiently!

Once you have created your content and loaded your images, spend some time formatting them. I use a plugin called YoastSEO to quickly scan my content and make recommendations on how to improve it for better SEO. Yoast will tell me if I've included my keywords enough, if I need additional headers, and if the post is considered long enough and readable. Who better to tell you if computers can read your content than another computer!

Once you have all your details, images and content in place, you can quickly schedule the time and date for your post to go live. I usually time my blog posts to go live just before my social media posts so that any traffic back to my website will see a consistent campaign.

Missinglettr

Missinglettr is a tool that creates automated social media campaigns to drive traffic for you all year long. It leverages blog post content to create strategic social media campaigns out of the content you've written. It can be a real timesaver if you want to focus on creating quality blog posts and let Missinglettr focus on teasing out the relevant social media posts.

Missinglettr connects to your website and monitors it for new blog posts. When they go live, Missinglettr will create potential social media posts and notify you to approve them. You have control over what goes out the door, while the heavy lifting is done for you. One thing to note is, if you choose to use this strategy, you have to focus on quality blog posts that is on target with your goals and themes to ensure that your overall marketing features relevant, quality content in line with your promotions.

Productivity

All of the tools, tips, and strategies featured throughout the book have been intended to help you become more efficient and productive in your work or personal life. Work-life balance is the art of juggling priorities and coming out unscathed. We all have different strategies and ways to make productivity more a part of our life. For some of us, it's about letting go of items that aren't actually a priority. For others, it's about recognizing where we are inefficient and making better use of that time. Being productive is often something we talk about, like it's an innate skill, but it's actually a learned art. We can learn to become more productive and to make better use of our time, but it takes practice like anything else.

Create a Top 3 List

As I've mentioned earlier in the book, I use a Top 3 system to ensure I cover key tasks each day. At the end of the day, I make a list of the Top 3 items I have to get done the next day to make it a success. I make these specific tasks, like narrate the webinar, or write three chapters. It has to be something finite that I can accomplish. Tasks like "work on the webinar" or "write the book" are too broad and end up getting pushed to the wayside when more quantifiable tasks come up.

I don't do anything fancy for my Top 3 list; I just grab a post-it and jot down the three items. The next morning, I dive in and start with this list to kick off my day. It makes sure I don't let key items slip through the cracks and ensures I start my day with the most pressing matters that will impact my success.

Focused work with Pomodoro

One of my favorite strategies that inspires and assists with productivity is leveraging the Pomodoro technique. This technique postulates that our brains can focus well for twenty-five minutes before needing a break. If we don't give ourselves a dedicated break, our mind tends to wander and we get distracted.

While I'm sure everyone's particular zone of focus can vary, I do find that I can be far more productive if I focus on a cycle of work and break. I personally use an application on my phone called Move On. It prompts me to enter a task and then start a timer. The timer runs for twenty five minutes unless I've adjusted it up or down, and then rings a timer and prompts me to take a break. When the timer rings again after a 5-minute break, it, again, prompts me and asks what I want to focus on. This system of identifying a single task I want to accomplish and working on it in a focused way for a short time is the secret sauce of my success. I call it "micro-tasking."

I use this all day long, starting with a focus on my Top 3 things for the day.

80/20 Strategy to Get Things Done

Another strategy that makes its way into almost all of my conversations is the 80/20 rule of thumb. This states that 80% of the time you work fast and hard and get the work done and out the door. 20% of the time, you need to focus on the details and make sure it's perfect. Blogging, creating video content, writing social media posts, there are going to be occasional typos, mistakes or broken links. You could stay in draft mode indefinitely fidgeting with the text and layout to get things just right, but in the meantime, you are missing sales. You need to push the go button and get that content out the door.

However, 20% of the time, you need to focus on the details. A printed marketing piece, a proposal to a client, a webinar gearing up for a major campaign...the details matter! Don't get me wrong, do your best at all times. But the point here is, don't let perfectionism stop you from putting things out. 80% of the time, getting the item to market is more important than the perfect layout, perfect font, or perfect words.

This happens in our personal life too. How often do you stay up late trying to get the house perfectly cleaned? If kids are going to wreck it again the next morning, do you really need to sacrifice sleep to make it perfect? Next time perfectionism is holding you back, think about the 80/20 rule and decide if that activity falls in the 80 or the 20 and cut yourself some slack. You are chasing balance after all!

Toby To Quick Launch Repetitive Tasks

I use a browser extension called Toby to help me quickly launch key tasks. Toby saves a specific set of tabs in your browser so you can relaunch them in the future. Every time I get ready to write a newsletter, I have several things I do. I open my email marketing program, a headline generator for ideas, my Content Creator Wizard for my newsletter and promotion content, and Canva for my graphics. In Toby, these are all saved under the task "Write an Email Newsletter" and I can click that task and it opens all of the tabs I just listed. I have Toby Tasks set up for all sorts of tasks I do frequently, like blog research, Social Media scheduling, meal planning, homeschooling and more. It's a great tool to help you bookmark tasks by the way you use them instead of just as a static list. You can find a link to Toby on our book bonuses page.

As tools go, this is a short list of a few of my favorite picks that focus on making you more productive and efficient. As with any tool, they only work if you use them, so be sure you use the right tool to solve a problem you're having.

Set it up and put it to work for you. Many of these tools are designed to work in the background, making your more efficient and productive with very little additional effort.

THE ART OF BALANCE

Is Work-Life Balance a Myth?

Can we really find balance? When I started writing this book, it had a completely different, quite boring title, but as I began getting closer to finishing it and started telling others about it, I had to explain what it was about. I had to develop an elevator pitch for it, something where I could tell its story in 90 seconds or less. The more I talked about it, the more it became clear that it was about chasing balance, pursuing priorities and leveraging tools and technology to find balance in today's digital world.

There are a few common misconceptions about work-life balance that seem to come up over and over.

One is the belief that only women are looking for it. Balance, that elusive promise, is the Holy Grail for many who think that once we treasure hunt, locate and embrace this concept of balance, our lives will be magically delicious. The problem is, balance is not static. It's a dynamic practice of shifting priorities and constantly juggling to find that sweet spot where things align. Since our priorities constantly shift, our balance needs to shift as well. The book is titled Chasing Balance because we are constantly moving in the direction of balance. You can't stop moving or your shifting priorities will overset you.

Balance comes from within. It is the acceptance of your state, whether that is as a person, a parent, an employee or an entrepreneur. We must pursue balance for the right reasons. The journey is where we find it. Identifying what is important to you, what your priorities are, and working to align your priorities and your goals...that is when we find our balance. Whether you need to scale back, ramp up, say yes, say no, finding balance is uniquely a personal journey and is different for everyone.

So, what do I hope you take away from this book?

I hope you build a schedule and recognize that it's a structure meant to support, not restrict you. Use your calendar to manage your work and personal priorities and ensure you make time for what is important to you.

Get up, get dressed, and pretend you are going to the office. Your commute may have shrunk to 15 seconds, but you are still going to work. It will be much less tempting to turn on the TV and channel-surf while you work if you are dressed up and at your desk at a normal working time.

Establish office space. Having a place for your office supplies, your computer, and for you to productively work will help make you more productive and give you somewhere to "leave" at the end of the work day.

Don't work weekends. Unless it's an emergency and you would be going into the office to handle it, or you run a business where you need to work weekends, don't work after hours and on weekends from home. If you do, co-workers will get used to having you available at all hours and will not hesitate to call. A polite but firm, "I'll handle that when I get to the office tomorrow" should let them know that you are offline and no longer working if they manage to catch you.

Work hard, but recognize that you are working. A lot of new telecommuters have trouble rationalizing not working crazy hours since they are at home. They take a break to throw in laundry or set a crockpot for dinner and see it as a reason to need to work overtime. However, in an office, co-workers would take a coffee break or visit over cube walls without feeling the need to work extra. Cut yourself some slack, take a normal amount of break time and then get back to work so you can confidently call it quits at the end of the day.

About the Author

I'm Traci, founder of MentoringU, long time work-at-home mom to three amazing children. After years in the corporate world, juggling work and home life, I craved a little work-life balance. And I wasn't alone! I was surrounded by other moms, entrepreneurs, single-parents, and small business owners desperate for more. MentoringU is a resource for entrepreneurs, bloggers, freelancers, and small business owners in search of training, tools, and guidance to help them grow their business. I offer trainings on building a website, managing social media, leveraging free small business resources, designing ads like a pro, using Google and Facebook ads, and leveraging the power of tech to get more done in less time.

When I began working with small business owners, it seemed like they felt the need to learn how to do everything themselves. They wanted to learn how to build their own website because they couldn't really afford a website designer to do it for them. They wanted to learn how to design their own graphics and use Photoshop. They wanted to learn how to manage their social media pages and how to design the cover art. They wanted to know how to set up email accounts and manage their accounting and invoicing. The list went on and on, and there was never enough time to do it all.

It's hard to find balance when you are trying to do everything yourself. MentoringU is a collaborative effort that helps fast-track small business owners by providing resources and launch materials to help them beat the obstacles holding them back.

Over the last 15 years, I have worked in various roles on projects of all sizes and scopes. I have worked in design, recruitment and implementation of grassroots programs, organized an extensive number of events, coordinating all aspects from planning through execution and post-event reporting, and successfully launched 3 businesses of my own, in addition to supporting numerous clients on their journey.

I am a champion of social media tools and technologies, with a consistent track record of creating and implementing successful training courses for program participants on incorporating and leveraging social media. I keep up to date with constantly evolving technologies and Web-based tools, and uses these skills to work closely with clients to create innovative, effective additions to their business offerings.

Chasing Balance Book Bonuses

Throughout the book, I've mentioned several downloads and resources that you can access to help you find balance in your work and personal life. To get access to these, register and access your resources at www.chasingbalancebook.com/bonus.

If you have any issues accessing your bonuses, please email hello@mentoringu.org.

Pursuit of work-life balance will inevitably give light to our priorities. Balance can only be achieved if we listen to what is revealed.

~Traci Synatschk

www.chasingbalancebook.com